Dad is...

Robin Willison

ISBN: 978-1-291-77054-4

PublishNation, London

www.publishnation.co.uk

For my wife Anna, our children, and their children

Introduction – it is worth reading this!

Why am I writing this book when I've never attempted to before?

I guess my motivation comes from two things. Firstly I've wanted to have a go at writing something for a while now and never got around to it – a few months off between jobs has given me the opportunity to have a go.

More importantly, the subject I want to tackle is both something I feel passionately about and where I have some experience to draw upon – being a Dad. It's also a subject where there seems to be surprisingly little written material giving practical help and guidance compared to, say, business related subjects such as 'Teamwork' or 'Managing Change'. Perhaps this is telling us that people are far more interested in business (or anything else for that matter) than fatherhood?

Be that as it may, the underlying proposition of this book is that a Dad DOES make a profound difference to the present and future well-being of his children (and also to the mother of those children). In saying this I'm not making an automatic judgment on situations where a father is absent. I'm also not saying that it's impossible to bring up children to become well-adjusted individuals, secure in their own worth and capable of building healthy and lasting relationships without a Dad being present.

What I am saying is how men do or don't fulfil their responsibilities as a Dad will make a big difference to their children – and most of us have a choice as to how much we put into fulfilling these responsibilities.

What this book is about, or rather who this book is for, is the man who accepts this and wants to do the best he can as a Dad – nothing more, nothing less. You may be a Dad to be or you may have had children for many years – it's never too late to try and be a better Dad. You just need to recognise how important you are to your children and be prepared to take honest and sometimes brave steps to fulfil your key role in their lives.

I have four children – they're wonderful, lovely. Not perfect, but siblings that love each other and their Mum and Dad, and make me proud every day. I've had something to do with how they've turned out – well, probably quite a lot along with my wife, Anna, and I will draw on my own experiences both good and bad as I write. But one thing I have learned as a parent is that the longer you have children the more you find that you don't have all the answers yourself. The moment I think I do is normally the time I'm about to fall flat on my face!

That's why this book isn't a manual of how to be a Dad. I don't want to tell you what **I** think; I want to help **YOU** think about how you can be the best Dad you can be. To help do that I've tried to find a structure that reflects some key principles of fatherhood as well as providing a discipline to ensure I present a balanced view rather than going off on any particular hobby horse of mine! The one I've chosen has worked for me and I hope it will for you. This is how I got to it:

At the heart of being a father is love, and one of the most familiar definitions of love is the one many of you will have heard, probably at a wedding ceremony. It goes like this:

Love is patient, love is kind. It does not envy, it does not boast, it is not proud. It does not dishonour others, it is not self-seeking, it is not easily angered, it keeps no record of wrongs. Love does not delight in evil but rejoices with the truth. It always protects, always trusts, always hopes, always perseveres. Love never fails.

Great words to ponder and to try to practice in our lives, but try substituting 'Dad' for the word love – it's suddenly a lot closer to home:

Dad is patient
Dad is kind
He doesn't envy
He doesn't boast
He isn't proud
Dad doesn't dishonour others
He's not self-seeking
He's not easily angered
He keeps no record of wrongs
Dad doesn't delight in evil but rejoices with the truth
Dad always protects
Always trusts
Always hopes
Always perseveres
Dad never fails

And for those of you who like to visualise things, here's a diagram to help you get your head around the structure of this book. It illustrates the twin foundations of patience and kindness and we'll see how much these two qualities run through all the other behaviours.

The 'Does Nots' and 'Is Nots' if read without the 'not' is a great list of Dad behaving badly. The Dad being an idiot list: Dad envies, Dad boasts, Dad's rude etc.

It all builds up to the 'Always' behaviours and is finally capped off with 'Dad never fails':

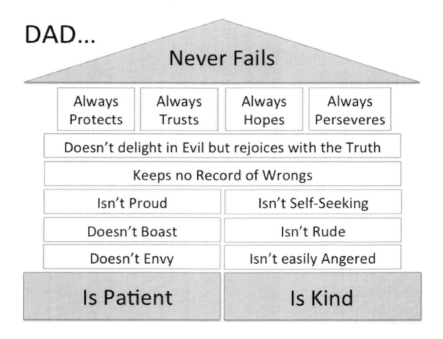

Now your first reaction to this may be – if that's the standard I'll never get there! However, please go with it for now and why not aim high anyway? Some of it will stick and it doesn't take much to make a big difference to your children.

I have devoted a chapter to each 'Dad Definition' – 15 may seem a lot but they are all short enough to read in 10–15 minutes at a time so I don't feel too guilty about adding in another one as important background before you get started.

Some of you will prefer to read a book from cover to cover but I know there will be others who want to dip in to chapters that you think may be immediately relevant or interesting. For you, I've put a brief summary of what each chapter is about on the contents page and hope that helps as a useful signpost.

I've included questions or suggestions for action for you to think over being mindful of Einstein's definition of insanity – 'Doing the same things and expecting something different to happen'. Please take time over these and perhaps talk them over with someone you trust and certainly your partner.

This book has been written for Dads but most of the time there will be two parents involved and how you work together is a fundamental element in how your children will grow up, even if you don't live together in the same house any more. Mum – please feel free to read this book and challenge Dad about what it says!

And finally…

Being a Dad has got to be one of if not the biggest responsibility and privilege any man can have. If there's anything you should want to do your very best at it's being a Dad to your children. You can and do make a difference – a life-changing difference – and I hope this book helps you in some way to do just that.

Robin Willison
January 2014

P.S. I'm afraid there are no answers in here about how to get them to turn the lights off!

Acknowledgements

It's always difficult to single out people to thank because of the risk of missing someone! But my special thanks must go to my friends Alan and Ray who made a particular effort to provide detailed feedback, together with the work of Anna and the children to ensure my anecdotes remained truthful!

Also to my son-in-law Phil for the cover design and to Julie who has been asking 'How is the book going Robin?' every time I've seen her during the six years since I mentioned I would have a go at writing it.

And finally to my own Dad who is no longer with us but who taught me so much about the power of patience and kindness, not just as a Dad but also in life.

Contents

7.   **Dad isn't proud**

About how the inflexibility of pride can damage relationships, but that there is still the greater power of saying sorry.

8.   **Dad doesn't dishonour others**

About respecting your children and how that teaches them the value of this vital foundation for any relationship.

9.   **Dad isn't self-seeking**

About putting your children first without making them think they are the centre of the universe!

10.   **Dad isn't easily angered**

About when anger harms but also when it helps.

11.   **Dad keeps no record of wrongs**

About the releasing power of forgiveness.

12.   **Dad doesn't delight in evil but rejoices with the truth**

About how discipline and praise prepares your children for life.

Dad never fails – Part 1

I've jumped right to the last of our 'Dad Definitions' before I even start tackling the rest, purely because one thing we can be absolutely sure of as a Dad is that there will be times when we fail.

I don't think that's what 'Dad never fails' means, and I'll explain more in the final chapter. But in the meantime let's assume that we will mess up and there's a danger that you could feel even worse about this when reflecting on how well you match up to each of the 'Dad is...' descriptions.

That's not the point of the book; it's not an instruction manual about how to be a Dad – of me telling you how to behave. It is meant to challenge your thinking on parenting and on some subjects you will decide to disagree; that's absolutely fine because all of our children and situations are different. However, at least you will have thought about it.

But when you do feel like the worst Dad in the world (as we can all do from time to time) I'd encourage you to remember three things:

1. Your children have an amazing capacity to forgive particularly when we say sorry.

2. We never stop learning as Dads and mistakes remind us of that!

3. You are not alone – for every one Dad who thinks he's doing a great job there are thousands who don't. And for

every Dad there will usually be a Mum who feels the same way.

That's one of the reasons why talking about and supporting each other as parents is a vital part of a relationship between Mum and Dad. However, you may also find it useful to discuss these difficult challenges with some trusted friends – not instead of but as well as with your partner.

Here's an idea: Why not invite a few friends round to talk through your challenges as Dads? You will not only learn from each other – what's worked and what hasn't – but it will also enable you to hold each other accountable for what you said you would try. It may even become a regular date for you – a time with Dads for Dads.

Something similar happened in Australia a few years back specifically for Dads whose marriages had broken up. Their website 'Dads in Distress' tells the story like this:

From a small meeting on a veranda in Coffs Harbour over nine years ago a group of Dads in distress met. We didn't know what we were doing only that we couldn't find any help for our circumstances. We met in the 'empty time' on a Sunday night after we had returned our children after weekend access and faced the coming fortnight alone without them.

It was there we shared our pain...sitting there on the veranda, telling our story and listening to others gave us hope for the future. We simply allowed each person to have his say without interruption, without giving advice and without judgment. Somehow that process provided the relief we all needed.[i]

You don't need to be in crisis to need and value that type of support and encouragement, to have our perspective changed through the mutual and encouraging support of other men just like us.

A year or so back and a bit closer to home, I was invited to a business dinner for some like-minded individuals who were trying to explore new ways of working together. What none of us expected was for the conversation to be dominated by us sharing experiences about being a Dad.

We all still remember and value that evening as it showed how important it is just to talk about these things.

We'll come back to support networks later on, but in the meantime why not start thinking about who you would trust to involve in an activity like this and then ask them? It's not difficult to set up so why not have a go?

Dad is there

Here's a story about priorities that had a big impact on me when I first heard it many years ago:

A lecturer at a business school was drawing his course to a close and to the surprise of his students suddenly reached down, took hold of a waste paper bin and put it on a desk. His audience really thought he had lost the plot when he THEN brought out a small sack of rocks from behind his podium and emptied them into the bin.

'Is the bin full?' he asked.

'Yes,' the students replied as one of the rocks over-balanced on the edge of the bin and fell with a crash to the floor.

'You're wrong,' the lecturer replied, and with that bent down to pick up a sack of gravel that he gradually tipped into the bin, shaking it gently, until the gaps between the rocks had been filled.

'Is it full now?'

'Probably not,' the students replied; after all they were an MBA class!

'Correct,' the lecturer replied as he picked up a bag of sand and proceeded to pour it into the bin to fill in the gaps that were left between the gravel and the stones.

Finally he took the jug of water on the podium and poured it into the bin, filling all the remaining gaps until the liquid started brimming over.

'It IS full now!' he said before asking, 'What's the moral of the story?'

Hands shot up in the front row and a young man shouted out, 'It doesn't matter how busy you are as you can always find time to do more.'

The lecturer smiled, 'No, that's NOT the moral of the story! The moral of the story is this:

'IF YOU DON'T GET THE ROCKS IN FIRST YOU WILL NEVER GET THEM IN.'

What are the rocks in your life, the things that are REALLY important to you? Possibly, more to the point, what is the gravel and sand that gets in the way of you getting around to those rocks?

Here's a suggestion – spending time, quality time, with your children.

You can read this entire book but if you don't spend time with your children it will be worth nothing. Being there isn't in our 'Dad is' definition, but without your physical presence you will never get an opportunity to have much of an influence on them.

This may sound obvious, but one of, if not the main obstacle to being an effective Dad is the amount of time we spend with our children. So why if it's SO obvious do SO many of us let other things get in the way SO often?

I really enjoy Rob Parson's books – they're so quick and easy to read but more importantly they burn certain observations or phrases into your mind forever! One of these in his *The Sixty Minute Father* book was this:

No one was ever heard to say on their death bed, 'I wish I had spent more time at the office.'[ii]

But the evidence often indicates quite the contrary! Early on in my career in business someone (I wish I could remember who) said to me:

'Remember, Robin, work has no morals – it will take you for what it can get. The only one who can say "No" is you.'

I cannot overestimate the value of that advice because when it comes down to making room for what's really important – the rocks in our lives – the responsibility sits squarely with ME. I can make as many excuses as I like about demanding bosses, job security and the like, but the truth is that I have the last word when it comes to the way I spend my time.

Here are a few ideas and observations I've picked up or practiced over the years that may help you to get practical with these challenges:

1. Communicate – I really do understand about the challenges of balancing a busy career with life at home, but one of the first things I learned was to make sure I communicated about this with my wife, Anna. Working together, I have found that we can make the times I do spend at home as productive as possible. It also helps us to share expectations so we don't get disappointed or frustrated with each other.

Something that worked for us was for me to agree to leave work at least twice a week in time to get home for an evening meal and bedtime with the family. One of these was normally a Friday but you'll find that your 'world of work' doesn't fall apart if you're not there after five or six o'clock one day in the middle of the week. Be careful to ensure that 'agree' includes your boss and colleagues as well as your partner – very often you'll find they are in the same position and, who knows, you may even start a trend.

This won't always work for the best of reasons but if occasionally you find you do have to stay on one of the 'early evenings' make sure you tell your partner as soon as you can.

This works both ways of course with Mums as well as Dads having busy working lives, so there will be a number of diaries to coordinate and compromises to be made. Also, circumstances change over time and sometimes quite quickly so it's wise to review what's been agreed regularly to ensure that quality time with your children doesn't suffer inadvertently.

2. Beware of bad habits – we all have super-busy periods at work but let's be honest, it's not always at that pace. It may be necessary to put in considerably longer hours from time to time but make sure that doesn't become the norm when it doesn't need to be.

3. A good intention remains a good intention until it gets in the diary – and that includes your commitments at home as a Dad. Make sure that the first thing you do when the school calendar comes out is to agree the 'must attend' dates and make sure they're in your work as well as home diary. Again, communicate about these things with your partner and your children so as to avoid disappointments.

When my eldest daughter went to university she put together a book of photos and written memories for us including a page for me that amongst other things said, *you never missed a sports day.* That meant more to me than any work appraisal.

4. Don't just be there, be REALLY there – it's not much good being home if you're mind is still in the office. Being there is about the quality as well as the quantity of time with our children, and one of the biggest piles of sand pushing out this particular rock is EMAIL.

If you do nothing else as a result of this chapter please switch off your email and your phone when you get home – at least for a couple of hours when you are with your children. Rob Parsons talks about 'listening with your eyes' and that's so true. Come to think of it, keep your devices switched off right into the evening, as your wife will want some quality time with you as well.

I've also found increasingly that it's not just work email that gets in the way – we get cross enough when someone jumps a queue ahead of us but seem to let Facebook, Twitter and even personal browsing push their way into our lives just as rudely without any comment. This is what we need to do:

SWITCH IT OFF!

The sand of email will have plenty of time to find its way into the gaps between your rocks. Just don't let it get there first.

And finally…

What do our children remember about their childhood? What do you remember?

When I ask my children they invariably talk about people – family, friends, teachers – rather than things. What memories are you building **WITH** your children? This may sound obvious but it needs to be said:

YOU need to be **WITH** them to do that. A Dad who is there.

What will change?

I said I would have a section like this at the end of every chapter simply because it's all very well to read this book and even agree with it, but nothing will change unless we decide to do something. You can decide to take action yourself or after talking with your partner, but as I said earlier it may also be useful to discuss your challenges with some fellow Dads.

Take time to write down what you want to do or change, or type it into your PDA – whatever works for you. I've also included some questions or activities that may help you get started. Here are the ones for this chapter:

1. What are the rocks in your life?

2. What are the rocks in your diary this week? Do these align with your answers to question 1?

3. If you employ child-care you will have taken great care to ensure both you and your partner understand who needs to be where and when. Have you used the same diligence in planning the time you both spend with your children?

4. Get hold of the school diary and talk through with your child what they want you to get to. Then get it into your work as well as your home diary!

5. Who do you feel comfortable asking to join and support you in this challenge to be the best Dad you can be? Give them a call.

6. Switch it off!

Dad is patient

So what do we mean by 'Dad is patient'? Here are a couple of dictionary definitions of patience to get started with:

1. *The ability to suppress restlessness or annoyance when confronted with delay.*

2. *The state of endurance under difficult circumstances.*

Do they sound familiar? When it comes to being a Dad they probably will, as the truth is that:

Our children will make mistakes and be slow to learn and invariably in those areas that annoy us the most!

But remember back to when they were first learning to walk – just think of the patience you had! What was your reaction the first time your precious little child set off from the safety of your supporting hands towards a grinning Mum cooing encouragement – and promptly landed flat on their face?

Did you walk away in disgust muttering: 'You're useless; I won't tell you again; keep moving; arms out; balance for goodness sake!' Of course not! You picked him or her up, gave them a cuddle and tried again – countless times – or just decided it was a bit too early. No worries or pressure (apart from the fact that their superhuman best friend has been walking since nine months) as you knew with time and patience that they would walk.

So what happens when they're in their teens and the smallest indiscretion sets us off on a rant about defiance and 'where did

I go wrong' mixed in with threats of grounding and pocket money docked for weeks on end? **Where did all that PATIENCE go?**

Where is the Dad who spent weekend after weekend bent double holding the seat of their child's bike as they learned the art of balance and the length of time it takes for grazed knees to heal? Is this the same man shouting bulge-eyed at the state of his son's room or the length (sorry, lack of length) of his daughter's dress? 'That's a nice belt, what about the rest?' What happens to us when we are confronted with our teenage offspring?

Seriously though, the patience of love **isn't** about whether we fly off the handle or not, although that does get covered later under Dad is slow to anger. Rather, it's about being brave enough to take the long-term view when it comes to our children.

I've sometimes heard this called the **'helicopter view'** – you see the whole of a journey from way up there and not just the ground level perspective of the little bit that's immediately in front of you. The short-term pain of negotiating a steep slope is felt worthwhile once you have experienced the view from the top of the hill, but the man in the helicopter already sees that view and knows that those on the ground will get there. Patience is about taking the helicopter perspective so…

DADS, WE NEED TO GET IN THE HELICOPTER!

We're much more useful to our children up there than struggling along beside them interfering in every aspect of their lives and, frankly, just getting in their way.

Back to teenagers – I remember once reading or hearing something that went a bit like this:

Take a good look at your 11 year old – their sweet personality, that willingness to please, those polite manners – and commit them to memory because very soon that person will mysteriously vanish and not reappear again for close on ten years!

At no point in your child's development is it more important to be able to take the long view than when they are in their teens. Don't lose patience. As you boil up inside…

TRY TO REMEMBER WHO THE ADULT IS

If we cannot keep things in the right perspective what chance do they have?

So how does taking the long view – getting in the helicopter – make a difference to our children?

a) You or your child isn't under pressure to always get things absolutely right.

Getting close is usually plenty good enough! In golf 'playing the long game' is all about percentages. You don't try and hit every shot at the pin; sometimes you have no chance of getting that far anyway so you play a shot that gives you the best next shot. Some golfer friends tell me that when they putt from a distance they don't go for the hole but imagine a circle the size of a dustbin lid and go for that instead.

Seve Ballesteros was one of the world's greatest ever golfers but consistently found himself off the fairway in the long grass, sand or even up a tree! But his greatness was based on how he recovered from these mistakes. How many times do we find ourselves in the 'long grass' as Dads, watching all those perfect families walking calmly up the fairway to a textbook lie whilst we're left hacking away in the bushes? Please remember when you find yourselves in these situations that there is always the next shot!

And if you mess up the whole round there's always tomorrow. Golf has two objectives – the first is to get round and the second to do that in as fewer shots as possible. In parenting the first is the most important – by far.

b) It helps us to focus on what's really important.

What's immediately in front of you isn't necessarily the most important thing to address. If you pick up on everything a child does wrong your correction or displeasure will lose its impact. Choose the right battles.

Our son once responded to some criticism by saying, 'Come on, if you think that's bad look at what I could be doing!' He had a point although we didn't let him know that at the time!

A friend told me how he had been nagging his young son about cleaning out his guinea pig cage one Saturday. He made a start but after five minutes got distracted into playing with something else. My friend got him focused back on the task in hand but soon after found that the same thing had happened. His son when challenged looked him in the eye and said, 'Dad, I'm a 12 year old boy and this is the only job I've got to do today. What's the rush?'

As we will see later it is probably better to praise more often than to scold. To adapt a well-known line from the classic *The One Minute Manager* book...*Catch your children doing something right.*

Here's a question to ponder: How much of our discipline is based on what others may think rather than what we think is best for our children?

c) It provides your children with the right amount of slack to make and discover the result of their mistakes for themselves – they tend to learn better and faster that way. Don't be too fast to jump in to warn or rescue them where there is little or no danger. I'm not saying don't ever intervene, but just to make sure it's not your 'default setting'. You'll find me return to that phrase a fair bit in this book.

I remember counselling one of my daughters approaching an important set of exams to avoid dating any boys and especially one particular individual. It took about a week for her to start dating that boy and another week to stop! We could have leapt in and forbade her to see him but what could we have done? Lock her in her room? Left to her own devices she came to the same conclusion – and then went out with someone else almost immediately! The exams were fine.

d) It gives us hope – even when things seem really bad – and Dad always hopes.

So how do you get in the helicopter? I'm only going to suggest one way but it's the one that I think is most important:

TAKE TIME TO BUILD YOURSELF A SUPPORT NETWORK

I remember a colleague a few years back who didn't arrive at work one morning. Now that was unusual as he was always one of the first there helping his team prepare for the day ahead. He eventually came in at around midday, very apologetic and saying he had unexpectedly needed to take a half-day off. 'Why? I asked.

'We must be such bad parents,' he replied. 'We've just spent the morning in the library trying to find books on raising children.'

Of course, I went on to ask what had happened to lead them to that rather damning conclusion.

'Well since their early teens they've taken it in turns to empty and load the dishwasher.' (At this point, like me, your mind may have wandered to your own children and whether they even know what a dishwasher is.) 'It's never been a problem, but this morning they disagreed whose turn it was and ended up screaming at each other.'

After telling him how much in awe I was of them as parents, having trained their children to interact with a domestic appliance, I asked whether he thought this type of arguing between teenage siblings was normal or not. He didn't know, simply because he hadn't talked to anyone else about these types of questions before.

Now I'm certainly not advocating that you expose the frailties of your children to everyone you come across, but talking to others that you trust on a regular basis helps to give a real sense of perspective as well as providing some useful advice on how to tackle the challenges we face as parents.

Dads in particular aren't great at talking about these things, and that's why I've already suggested you make a habit of going for a beer with some friends to off-load to each other. You'll find it a real source of encouragement and it will also help you to stay patient and gracious with yourself – particularly when you're in the long grass!

What will change?

1. If you haven't done so already discuss with your partner about who you can talk to about your parenting challenges. You may decide to do that together, but it's still worth considering which other Dads you may want to meet with from time to time. Remember, a good intention remains a good intention until it gets in the diary.

2. Think of a time within the last few weeks where you intervened in a situation in your child's life. Be honest about what the result was. Could you have taken a different approach?

3. What are your long-term goals for your children? Something else to talk through with your partner.

4. Dig out some pre-secondary school pictures of your child and be encouraged that you will see that person again one day.

Dad is kind

I've found it quite challenging to succinctly define what kindness is, perhaps that's because its life-lifting impact is able to express itself in so many different attitudes and behaviours.

It's a bit like salt in that respect; you can eat food without it but seasoning applied with skill and care can make good ingredients taste great. Our kindness as a Dad seasons the lives of our children; not as occasional large applications but as regular little pinches every day in all that we do with them and for them.

In dictionary definitions of kindness, the word 'benevolent' keeps coming up: it's a desire to do good to others based on our love and respect for them as human beings. Kindness isn't just for special cases, it's for everyone we meet, but for our children the kindness of a Dad has a special and irreplaceable impact.

Kindness along with patience should be our defining characteristics as a Dad.

Some think that kindness is a sign of weakness – of being too soft – and kindness can often feel 'soft' to the recipient. There's nothing wrong with that at all but a kind act will sometimes need to be a firm one. I don't think you ever have to be 'cruel' but I know what the 'cruel to be kind' saying is getting at – the truth can sometimes be hard to take, but it's normally for the best in the long run.

However, there are ways of delivering correction that can be kind or unkind. Take our reaction to failure as an example.

Failure is real, it happens and we probably shouldn't dress it up as anything else. It is kind to support your child through failure, helping them to learn any lessons and give them hope for the future, but it's unkind to label or call them a failure, be that in words or in the way you treat them.

A person who can continue to respond with kindness under pressure – who can still be looking out for the best interests of even those who are creating the pressure – is the strongest kind of person.

'Random Acts of Kindness' has become quite a fashionable phrase over recent years inspiring activities like the 'One Million Random Acts of Kindness Campaign' on BBC radio in 2008, including 'The Kindness Offensive' where the Christmas event is cited by some as the UK's largest ever random act of kindness.

The concept has even got to Hollywood with the 2007 film, *Evan Almighty,* ending with God telling Evan that the way to change the world is by doing one Act of Random Kindness (ARK) at a time. Think of that what you will, but ARKs by Dads certainly change the world of their children.

I like the term 'random' because it brings out what is at the heart of true kindness; that it's unconditional not being in response to or in expectation of something beneficial to the giver. It is truly selfless and Dad is not self-seeking.

At its simplest it includes good old-fashioned manners; smiling and saying good morning to someone who catches your eye; letting someone go before you in a queue; taking the trouble to say thank you; saying sorry and meaning it. Dad doesn't dishonour others, or put another way, 'Dad isn't rude'!

Random acts of kindness can be small or large; a surprise room-tidy; a Valentine's Day breakfast for your daughter (and wife); the latest PlayStation game. There's nothing wrong with some of these being a celebration of something they have achieved or a reward for good behaviour, but what's really powerful is when that's got nothing to do with it – in other words it's entirely random.

I still remember the day we bought a trampoline for our children. Like many young families we didn't have much money at the time so this wasn't a normal occurrence. They were genuinely surprised and looked for reasons why we had done it; any birthdays soon, a good school report perhaps? 'No, none of these,' we replied. 'There isn't a reason. We just wanted to treat you.' We were also reminded of something else about kindness that day – that it gives as much pleasure to the giver as the receiver. Just look at what happened to Scrooge!

Kindness builds memories that stick, and in years to come you'll find your own children doing the same thing with their offspring. Unkindness can also stick and its damaging consequences replicated down the generations.

Kindness is generous – it is possible to 'spoil' your children but withholding kindness can spoil just as much. And generosity isn't just about things; it also encompasses time, praise and affection. Be generous with the time and attention you give your children. Remember this is one of your rocks and the sand of busyness is unlikely to get any less.

Kindness is merciful – how many times do you forgive your child? As many times as they need forgiveness because Dad keeps no record of wrongs – that's a really challenging one and will get its own chapter.

Kindness is also tender – we've come a long way from the emotional starvation of the Victorian age, but the inability to establish an emotional connection – even simply to tell your children you love them – is still a massive issue for some Dads.

It's not just about words as loving kindness can express itself in many ways and there is plenty of truth in the saying 'actions speak louder than words'. But we mustn't let that become an excuse for not expressing our love to our children with simple words and a hug. Big 'squeezy hugs' from a child are also brilliant for unwinding stressed Dads!

Random acts of kindness are special but so are planned and habitual ones. Making a fuss of a birthday or planning a holiday full of children-focused memories and surprises becomes no less special if it happens every year. Even those endless unpaid taxi duties can be a special time; in fact, sometimes the only time you'll get a chance to nail your teenager down without them being able to get away from your conversation and questions! Never make them feel guilty about these rides. Believe me, you'll be grateful that their first reaction when they get into trouble on a night out is to call their kind old Dad for a lift.

Kind, everyday reactions in the little things build a trust that tells your children that 'the door is always open' for them to come to you for help even when they really mess up. And true kindness is what really kicks in when the going gets tough; when our children probably least deserve it and when we feel the least inclined to be kind, because:

Our children need to know that however hard or far they fall that they will always have the kindness of Dad to land upon.

And finally...what is the reason for our kindness?

I remember giving a talk where I took a bit of a risk by involving my four year old son without him knowing or being prepared in advance. I called him up to the front and asked him to stand on a chair so everyone could see him. 'Jack,' I asked, 'why do I love you?'

Without any hesitation he answered, 'Because you're my Dad.'

As we express our kindness in planned as well as random ways, it underlines to our children why we love them; **not because of anything they may or may not have done but because of who they are**. Our children.

Kindness is a driving passion to do the very best for our children. It will let them know that we care so much for them and that they are highly valued. It will make them feel special because they are – because they belong to us.

What will change?

1. Tell your children you love them today – and keep telling them!

2. Plan something kind for your children today – have you got those important events from the school calendar in your diary yet?

3. Kindness isn't just for your children – plan something kind, even spontaneous for your partner. Your children get huge amounts of pleasure seeing the evidence of their Mum and Dad in love – however much they may deny it!

4. Can you think of any unkind things you may have said or done to your children? It's never too late to say you're sorry and you'll be amazed how forgiving your children will be when faced with a truly repentant Dad. They probably cut us a lot more slack than we do for them!

Dad doesn't envy

Envy and jealousy are extremely uncomfortable, based upon negative experiences such as insecurity, low self-esteem, feelings of inferiority, loneliness, distrust, fears of loss, suspiciousness, ill will, resentment, bitterness or anger, often accompanied by shame and guilt. Allowing these negative experiences certainly puts you in the power of the green-eyed stress monster. **Betty W. Phillips, PhD, Psychology** [iii]

Oh dear – this subject sounds serious! And she goes on to say that these experiences start right back in childhood with our child's need for attention and security; clearly the way we help them to deal with these issues will have a significant impact on preparing them to manage envy and jealously as they grow up into adulthood.

The words 'envy' and 'jealous' tend to be used interchangeably but what we will be talking about specifically here is the desire to have something that someone else has. We can all recognise some of the results: a 'chip on the shoulder'; people thinking 'the world owes them something'; an inability to feel pleasure in the success of others.

It can be about material things: appearance, intelligence, achievement, relationships – the list goes on and on – but its roots are very similar, and the quote at the top of the page makes a pretty comprehensive list!

The truth is that the green-eyed envy monster can eat you up

I want to cover three things in this chapter: a Dad's envy of his child, his envy of other Dads and helping your child with envy. In doing so we shall recognise the twin antidotes of contentment and gratitude.

1. Dad doesn't envy his own children

This is quite common amongst Dads particularly around the time of our 'first-born', but very few of us talk about it. Not surprisingly we find ourselves dealing with jealous thoughts, whilst at the same time experiencing shame and even revulsion at the way we feel.

Before your child came along you were pretty much the centre of your partner's life. She gave you her attention in the evenings and at the weekends, she was full of energy (well most of the time) and interested to do things with you. Making love was a regular part of your life together. Then seemingly overnight – although let's face it the signs were there for at least nine months – there is someone else taking all of her attention and energy. You've become a sideshow.

These feelings can become even stronger when you are prevented in some way from embracing your role as a Dad. In-laws, aunts and uncles always about, and sometimes even an overprotective new Mum.

Here are two suggestions that may help during this wonderful but challenging period:

- Focus on being parents together.
- Communicate with each other about what you're feeling.

One of the more significant and helpful government initiatives in recent years has been the introduction of paternity leave. I never had that but it must be a wonderful opportunity to do all these new child things together – that's what you've always enjoyed, doing things TOGETHER – and now here's something completely new and exciting to experience TOGETHER again.

Use this time wisely to develop routines, to appreciate the common and different roles you now have in caring for your child. And talk about how you're BOTH feeling. The reason why your partner seems to be giving so less time is possibly a coping mechanism for coming to terms with the invasion of her own time and privacy by the new arrival. She won't put it that way because she wouldn't have it any other way, but the last thing she needs is another child to deal with – you!

However, it can be all too easy for new parents to let what should be short-term adjustments become unhelpful habits and that's why you need to talk. Giving exclusive quality time to each other is an important discipline, and although we may inwardly cringe at the term 'date nights' they do work for many. You have space to talk and enjoy one other's company, to make each other feel special. But these times need to be planned and not least involve finding a baby-sitter you can trust. So, at the risk of being boring, please remember: a good intention remains a good intention until it gets in the diary!

And finally here – beware. The period following the birth of a child is a classic high-risk one for a man looking elsewhere for affection and excitement. The only one who can deal with this challenge is you and there are no excuses for straying – you're a Dad as well as a partner now, and what can be a phase in life that is as difficult as it is joyous is only a phase. Take the helicopter view!

2. Dad doesn't envy other Dads

You are the best Dad your child could ever have! Other Dads may have plenty to offer – expensive holidays, time on their hands, DIY skills to pass on – but they aren't you!

You need to get hold of this truth and live it day to day. Certainly we're far from perfect, but so is everyone else's Dad even if your child keeps talking about how wonderful one or more of them is.

Are you content with who you are and with what you have? If you're not the likelihood is that you will pass this attitude onto your children. There may be some very good reasons why you envy others – lack of self-esteem, knocks you have taken in life, insecurity through the lack of or even absence of parental love. These are powerful influences but they can be overcome even if it takes a professional to help you.

It is up to you though – if what you think about yourself is a real problem take the initiative to seek help. But if it's something that only comes up from time to time, just try choosing to think differently when it does. You need to understand that here is something that you can give that no one else can give:

YOUR LOVE

YOUR child needs to know YOUR love in regular and practical ways and that's why we need to give time to them.

Here we are, back at 'Dad is there', but absence is at the root of so many problems in parent–child relationships.

Don't try and be someone else. Be yourself. Find something you BOTH enjoy doing together. Anyone can come up with random acts of kindness and they don't even need to cost any money – time is far more valuable than money, but, as we've already said, it does need to be planned as well as impulsive. Sit down and tell your children about your childhood; read them a story, go conker collecting, cook a meal together and rave about what they produce as if it's the most delicious thing you've ever tasted!

Your child doesn't want another Dad, they want you; your affection, your unreserved positive regard, your kindness, your time. And if they talk about someone else's Dad in glowing terms, join in their delight and admiration. That way they will learn to feel secure enough to think the same about their friends and to understand that although you cannot have it all, you can have enough to be content with who you are.

Most of all they will be content and grateful to have you as their Dad.

3. Dad helps his own child to deal with envy

Coping with your own temptation to envy others is a great place to start as your children will mimic what you do. It also puts you in a good place to build the foundations of contentment and gratitude in their hearts and minds. Here are some ideas about how to do this:

'I don't care too much for money, money can't buy me love' – be careful how much you focus on money and material things because John and Paul weren't far wrong! There are far more important things in life than building financial wealth. True, money can bring you more freedom to choose, but having a choice doesn't necessarily make you content. What's the point of spending so much of your time earning enough money to privately educate your children if they're strangers to you at the end of it?

Teach your children how to value diversity in others and themselves because no one person can have everything. As human beings we need each other, pooling our particular skills and characteristics to build something bigger and better. Who is more important in a football team, the goalkeeper or the striker? You need both of course.

There is a 'golden rule' here that is very easy to break if we don't watch ourselves – **be very careful about comparing your child with others.** If you do it to make them feel good you could be fuelling superiority and elitism, and if you're doing it to shame them into action they could be stuck with that performance-based motivation and perspective for life. It will also almost certainly damage their relationship with those you compare them against.

There's another side to this – don't lie to your child about themselves. There's nothing wrong with them being less gifted at sport or academically and them recognising that, but they do need to value themselves for who they are and if we support that process it makes it so much easier for them. If what defines us is our performance, the value of a human being would go up and down as much as any other commodity.

Our children are NOT a commodity and it's up to us to guide them on how to evaluate their immense and enduring value – and that DOESN'T involve comparison with others.

Help your children to feel good about who they are – not by comparing them but by kind words and actions of encouragement. I'm not saying that you eradicate ambition and aspiration, only that it's kept in the right perspective. Many of us are so focused on where we are going that we miss out on the beauty and joy of the journey itself. Teach your children to take time, to count their blessings, to be grateful for the people and things around them. Be generous with your appreciation of them and of others.

Avoid taking the cheap shot – Dad's love to be the funny one and perversely our children seem to enjoy the embarrassment of our dreadful jokes. But they don't enjoy jokes at their expense particularly when they know that we know it's aimed at a weak spot in their lives.

And finally...

It's never too early to start doing these things, and even if you've neglected them so far it's certainly better to start late than never. You can still make a huge difference.

When our child is a baby it's obvious what we are doing to protect and nurture them – if we leave them to their own devices they would quite simply die. As they grow older what we influence becomes less obvious, but if we don't take the same care to nurture and protect their minds and spirits as well as their bodies they can die inside.

In particular, the green-eyed envy monster can eat them away if we don't help them to feel good about themselves; to be content and grateful. Dad, you have the power to do that because Dad doesn't envy.

What will change?

1. Get those 'date nights' in the diary.

2. Try choosing to say something positive about someone instead of the criticism that so often first comes to mind. Believe me that's challenging, but it can make a real difference to your attitude.

3. Take a few minutes with your partner to write down some ideas of simple but fun things to do with your children. Rob Parsons' book, *The Sixty Minute Father,* has some great ideas in it and if you haven't got around to buying a copy yet you're missing out!

4. If you're struggling with envy yourself find someone to talk to about it.

Dad doesn't boast

I could come at this from a number of angles:

- 'When I was a boy…'
- 'Our Johnny is achieving so much at school…'
- 'You won't believe how great that meeting was today – I really nailed that deal…'
- 'I'm a great Dad – and those aren't my words but my children's!'

Very few of us will warm to a boastful man possibly because we know that as they 'big themselves up' they will at the same time be putting someone else down even if only by default. I'm not talking here about giving an honest assessment of your own or your child's achievements, but I think we all know when this crosses the line into bragging or crowing and that's when others will suffer.

A few thoughts concerning boasting about yourself:

Whatever the motivation and however annoying it is, the real problem with someone who spends all of their time speaking about themselves is that all the time they're doing that they're not listening to others.

The person who boasts sacrifices the long-term regard of the person you could have listened to for the short-lived gratification of their grudging appreciation because:

BOASTING CROWDS OUT WHEREAS HUMILITY MAKES SPACE.

Someone who makes an honest appraisal of their own talents and achievements as well as knowing when and not to talk about them makes room to listen to and learn from others around them. Our children not only need us to be around but also for us to pay attention to them, and one of the best ways to do that is to listen, really listen.

Now I know that when they get into their teens it's sometimes difficult enough to get them to talk in the first place, but when they do what will encourage them to do it again is if we listen – it's not about you, it's about them. We'll come back to that one.

I'm not sure there are many of us Dads who boast about how good we are at parenting. If we do boast we will almost certainly be brought down to earth with a bump at some point. If anyone is qualified to boast about our Dad skills it's our children, so leave it to them if you really think you're that good!

Children do learn through example so the way you talk about yourself or them – abilities, appearance, achievements, whatever – will help teach them how and when to talk about themselves. If you boast they will probably either do the same thing themselves or go to the other extreme and decide that they will never talk about what they have achieved. Neither will help them either as children, adults or eventually as parents themselves.

One area to avoid like the plague is talking up what you achieved as a child because even if you don't intend to make a comparison with your child, they will! Memories fade with time and what you remember in a warm glow of self-congratulation may not be a true representation of the facts.

Our children sometimes find it hard to separate the truth from the enhancements and tend to take what their Dad says at face value particularly when they are younger. So when they compare the glowingly spun truth of Dad's childhood years with the gritty and current reality of their own experience, its little wonder that they can end up feeling discouraged.

By all means tell stories about when you were young – I know that all my children loved to hear mine. Just make sure they are balanced and laced with plenty of self-deprecating humour!

So onto boasting about your children:

If you've never seen the Steve Martin film, *Parenthood,* I warmly recommend that you do. It's a bit dated now but includes some brilliant and timeless observations that are as funny as they are insightful.

One of my favourites is the parents with the highly intelligent child who seems to possess a wider vocabulary at the age of three than I do now. The Dad in particular was obsessed not only with driving his daughter onto even higher levels of intellectual achievement, but also taking every opportunity to boast about her to his wider family.

The little girl's boy cousin on the other hand lived in a world of his own and in one scene was walking around with a bin on his head, bumping into random objects. 'You must be so proud,' said the little girl's father to the father of the little boy.

Like that particular Dad, you just get a sense that some parents are motivated by living in the reflected glory of their children.

BUT IT'S NOT ABOUT YOU – IT'S ABOUT THEM

There are several reasons why you shouldn't boast about your children and you can probably come up with more, but here's a few to start with:

1. It almost certainly embarrasses them and makes them feel uncomfortable and this becomes more acute the older they get. I'm not talking here about genuine praise although I would counsel being careful about praising your children too much in public. A private and heartfelt word about how proud you are of them, and specifically what for, builds their confidence and self-worth without the complications of the reactions of others.

2. It could well make your child unpopular not just with their friends but also your friends. No one likes a 'smart-arse' and even if it's not your child boasting about their achievements the comments that you make somehow stick to them. It can also reduce the sympathy and support they may have had when the inevitable fall comes.

3. Your children will almost certainly not want to let you down and building up their achievements too much can leave them getting stressed with expectations that they just cannot fulfil.

4. As they tend to believe what you say, any exaggeration can become the reality in their own minds and that's dangerous if it's inaccurate. Never knowingly set your child up for failure.

5. We will come later to the essential place of praise that helps to build up the self-confidence and self-image of our children because Dad does rejoice with the truth. But that's very different from what we have just been talking about;

the occasional boast does little harm but a self-absorbed obsession with the promotion of yourself or your child can cause them serious damage.

6. So even if you are truly being motivated by a heart that's bursting with pride in your little darling, still make sure you stop and think before opening your mouth – what will the publicity you are about to seek really achieve?

What will change?

1. Why not write a short letter to your child to tell them what has made you proud of them over the past month or so. Read it out to them with just you and them and possibly your partner there.

2. Make time to tell your children stories about your childhood – perhaps ask your partner to be there to keep you honest!

3. How often do you speak about yourself? Try asking questions of the other person about them – and then listen to the answer!

Dad isn't proud

This isn't about pride in your children although we are proud even if we don't boast!

This is about the proud blinkers of the relationship world, a way in which you may perceive yourself or circumstances that ultimately causes you to fall. Pride really does come before a fall, but when you're a Dad it can be your children that fall over with you.

Pride at its worst is an unreasonable and inordinate self-esteem that is so serious that it even finds its way into the list of the Seven Deadly Sins! Here are four specific areas to help you think through how proud you are and what that could mean to both you and your children.

1. A Dad who isn't proud can keep an open mind

Every child that we are given is different both physically and psychologically. So why do so many of us have a rigid 'one size fits all' approach to parenting? Perhaps it's been shaped by how we were brought up, or by observing a family that we admire, or even from a parenting manual.

I remember attending a parenting course with my wife when our children were very little and it was really useful for us if only because it provided a regular discipline for us to talk together about how we were raising our children without interruption or distractions.

However, I can still remember one particular Dad who was very keen to tell us all in a discussion group what he thought was the best way to raise his family; a strong work ethic, private education; to play a musical instrument etc. I'm not knocking any of these but were all of his children the same? Would this work for each one of them?

It was also interesting to observe that this same individual had taken his cue from a particular part of the teaching input that reinforced his own view of parenting. It seemed that he was collecting evidence to substantiate his approach rather than keeping an open mind to other possibilities.

Was he proud? I think the symptoms of pride were there in that he was so sure that his way was correct that he just didn't seem to be teachable. He had thought it through and his way was the best and right way.

I know someone else who was excellent at encouraging his boy into extra-curricular activities like scouting, charity work and music and also to support that child when it became clear that he had leadership abilities and was being given responsibility in a number of these things. The father's encouragement did benefit his son greatly but he missed out on his boy's passion for sport simply because he wasn't particularly interested in it himself. 'I had no idea' were his words when he finally watched his son play a game, years later.

Dad – have the humility and patience to take time to understand the individual passions and abilities of your children and then make sure you weave these into the plans and aspirations you have for them.

It's useful to have a framework and a plan for how you approach being a Dad. It helps to prevent you drifting along with the lives of you and your children being buffeted about and controlled by external events and circumstances. However, if it's too rigid it can break – or rather break your children. Houses in a high-risk earthquake zone have flexibility built in; they need to be able to move with the tremors rather than simply resist them.

In the same way, as Dads we need to lay our pride aside and have the humility to be flexible; to admit we don't know it all and most of all to accept that we make mistakes.

2. A Dad who isn't proud can admit he is wrong

We've already touched on the 'Dad never fails' oxymoron and we know that it DOESN'T mean that we never make mistakes. But there's a big difference between recognising that we make mistakes and admitting that to our partner, friends or most importantly our own children.

Let's face it, we're not perfect as people and certainly not as a Dad. Your children also know you're not perfect particularly the older they get and most definitely when they hit their teens, but that doesn't mean they respect or love you less.

Dads, we must have the confidence to be able to show and share our frailties with our children, and particularly when it comes to mistakes we make that have affected them directly. For example, I cannot count the times I have flown off the handle at one of mine when I've been under pressure at work and lost perspective as a result.

When you're standing and looking at someone face to face you get a true perspective but when you're down at their feet looking up they look huge! Many things in life – tiredness, failure, whatever – can leave us on the floor looking up and when that happens we can so easily lose perspective and make mistakes. But when it does happen:

NEVER UNDERESTIMATE THE POWER OF SAYING SORRY.

A sincere apology is one of the most powerful antidotes for relationship pressure. How many families are there that have been split apart because of pride, because someone won't say that single simple word, or if another won't accept the apology, forgive and move on?

Confession of our mistakes and the response of forgiveness is the great healer for those on both sides of the incident or argument. Without it, relationships are like a machine without oil – they grate, make alarming noises and eventually just blow up and cease to operate. The power of saying sorry is one of life's greatest lessons and your children can learn it direct from Dad (and Mum of course)!

Showing and sharing your frailties with your children is very powerful – it also makes it a lot easier for your future son-in-laws when their darling daughter thinks about comparing their husband to their super Dad!

3. When a Dad isn't proud he can forgive his own child

We'll return to this subject when we consider 'Dad keeps no record of wrongs' but for the moment here's an all too common tragedy – a Dad who has cut off his own child.

Perhaps it's because of disobedience but the consequence will very probably be out of proportion to the 'crime' – 'If you drop out of university don't expect any more financial support from me,' or 'if you walk out that door don't bother coming back.' Sometimes you still live in the same house together but the Dad effectively ignores the child or is at best just coldly civil.

Can your child ever do anything that you cannot forgive? Surely there must be a line where it's just impossible to be reconciled? I'm not sure how useful that sort of question or discussion is except only to observe that the majority of family dislocation is down to events that are far less serious than whatever list of unforgiveable misdemeanours we can come up with.

If we're honest, pride is usually the only wall between estranged parents and children. The reason for the original falling out is often lost back in time and only left standing by the surrounding scaffolding of subsequent self-justification. I recently watched an episode of *Who Do You Think You Are* about John Simpson the well-known war correspondent. His closing words were as true as they were moving and for so many families:

> *'I felt dreadful that I had sided with my father against my mother and it kind of built up this tremendous burden of guilt – I think on both our parts – that kept us separate.*

> *'Now I'd just go straightaway. The worst thing is to know that it's too late.*

> *'I'm determined, absolutely determined to make sure that my family doesn't allow distances and separations to grow up because they don't do you any good. Don't let the gaps grow; shrink them.'*[iv]

Remember the helicopter? Our children and particularly teenagers find it hard to get into the helicopter; the heady combination of hormones, peer pressure and even parental expectation means that getting a healthy perspective isn't always possible. It's up to the parents to get in the helicopter, take the long-term view that helps us to take the first move to put things right, even when we didn't instigate things in the first place.

DAD – REMEMBER WHO THE ADULT IS BEFORE IT'S TOO LATE.

4. A Dad who isn't proud can learn

We never stop being a Dad and we should never stop learning how to be the best Dad we can be. If we think we know it all or just don't admit to our weaknesses and doubts first to ourselves and then to others, we won't learn. We won't get any better.

Joining a group of Dad mates, or even just one friend, to talk in confidence, to share our experiences and to ask for help can only happen if we take off the blinkers of pride. In fact, just the act of doing that will help us to take them off as we begin to realise that ours isn't the only way; that we can all learn, that we can laugh at ourselves and that saying sorry really works.

What will change?

1. Did anything in this chapter touch a raw nerve? Don't be too proud not to admit it. Think of ways to develop a productive humility and particularly when it comes to your relationship with your children.

2. Is there a distance in your relationship with one of your children at the moment because of something you have done; perhaps the way you have reacted to something that they have done? Try reaching out to them. Take the risk of saying sorry without strings and see what happens.

3. Talk to your children about what's important to them and then encourage and support them in those things. It may also help them to respond more positively to other suggestions from you perhaps less attractive to them at the time, but still good for them even though they may not realise that now.

4. Talk to your partner about your frailties and doubts as a Dad if you haven't done so already. Forgive each other and work through any disagreements you have about your children and anything else for that matter. Sorry shouldn't seem to be the hardest word!

Dad doesn't dishonour others

Some translations of the 'Love is…' definition use the words 'Love is not rude' so if you prefer it, 'Dad isn't rude'! Either way this is all about respect for others starting with your partner and children, but not only for them. It's at the heart of any relationship and without it you will never be able to build trust.

The common element of just about every dictionary definition I can find of respect is the word 'regard': to regard with special attention; to regard as worthy of special consideration or attention; to regard with honour. You're not likely to be rude to anyone you regard in that way; you're much more likely to treat them with patience and kindness.

Respecting your child

Of course we regard our children with special attention, as being worthy of special consideration, attention and honour. But do our actions reflect what we think we know and feel, and if they don't are we really being honest when we say we respect our children?

How can we dishonour our children? Here are a few thoughts:

- Do we really listen to them?
- Do we make giving them quality time a priority?
- Do we value their opinions? Do we even ask for them?
- Do we include them when other adults are about?
- Have we talked over them or told them to 'shut up'?
- Have we called them 'stupid' or worse?

- Have we grunted a bad tempered 'Good Morning' or just ignored them completely?
- Do we expose them to others in public or private in a way that embarrasses them?
- Do we discipline and correct them in public because of what others may think?
- Do WE remember to say 'please' and 'thank you' to THEM?
- When was the last time you barged into your teenager's room without knocking?
- Have you ever walked into the lounge and switched TV channels without asking when they're already watching?
- Have we ever excused our behaviour with the words or thought, 'you don't deserve any better'?
- Have we indulged their bad behaviour by failing to tell them the truth about what the consequences may be?

Speaking for myself I'm pretty close to collecting the full set and I'm sure many others of you will feel the same. However, what's really important isn't whether we have ever done these things but whether these behaviours represent our 'default setting'. If they are and we see nothing wrong we are rude fathers, plain and simple, and quite possibly rude men.

You've heard the expression, 'He doesn't suffer fools gladly'; there's a simpler way to say it. 'He's rude'!

Here's a personal view on respect – it should be based on who people are rather than what they have achieved or where they belong. All of us deserve equal respect because we are human beings; that's the starting point. You can admire what others have achieved or want to associate yourself with a particular set of beliefs or behaviours. However, the foundation of respect for a fellow human being should be where we start, even when they don't appear to respect us in return!

Now this is very challenging if we apply it to everyone, and it's not my place or the purpose of this book to persuade you of its validity as an approach to life. However, it's a lot easier to see how it applies to your children so let's stick to that for the time being.

Going back to the list above, a lot of these behaviours are unintentional and the result of thoughtlessness. A good place to start when we want to demonstrate respect is to think about the other person, to focus on our children and try to see things from their point of view, and when we do it should start to affect these areas:

a) Listening – when they come to you with questions or you ask them a question, try to shut off other distractions and give them all your attention. If it's not convenient tell them so (gently), perhaps explaining why but certainly saying when they will be able to have your time. Ask them questions to clarify what they mean and ask them if they've already had any ideas themselves. That's probably what we would do with a fellow adult so why not our children?

Sitting down together over a meal is often a really good way to give quality time and attention to our children, or perhaps on one of those countless 'taxi of Dad' journeys. Including our children in discussing 'big' family decisions like holidays, what we want to do at Christmas, moving house or even choosing schools will not only increase their sense of personal value, but also help teach them the key life skills of consensus and compromise in helping any group of people to function effectively.

b) Greeting – first impressions do count and not just the first time you meet someone. In a very real sense the start of every interaction is a mini 'first impression' and helps to set the tone for what follows. A smile or a hug makes a morning or an evening start so much better than a distracted grunt or a moan. If you have a dog take a lesson from the way they react when you walk in the room!

Children waiting at the window for your return or running to open the door will light up our hearts. Did you ever consider that a similar reaction to your child does the same for them? That doesn't mean to say you can hang around your front windows late at night waiting for your teenager to be dropped off - that would just be TOO embarrassing! In fact, and in all seriousness, it would be disrespectful to a child you trust.

c) Manners – exercising common courtesies is a simple way of demonstrating and communicating respect. At its heart is consideration for others so it is all about respect. Children are far more likely to mind their 'Ps and Qs' if they see their Mum and Dad doing just that, and particularly when THEY are treated like that by YOU.

Like so many things, if they learn it young it's a habit that will stick. They will also find that it endears them to people if it's a genuine and natural response. The Cub Scout Law has it right when it encourages young people to 'think of others before yourself'. Come to think of it, doing a 'good deed every day' isn't a bad idea either; acts of random kindness didn't start with *Bruce Almighty* after all!

d) Gossip – my father-in-law has a simple approach to this: 'If you cannot think of anything positive to say about someone, don't say anything.' In fact I watched Disney's *Bambi* the other day and discovered that Thumper the rabbit repeated this wisdom!

It's really easy to slip into discussions (and they're nearly always critical ones) about people behind their backs. That's not to say we gloss over issues where someone has behaved badly, but we try to steer these discussions towards resolving whatever the problem is. It's not a big leap for a child to listen to what their Dad is saying about someone else and for their thoughts to drift towards, *If that's the way he talks about them I wonder how he talks about me when I'm not around?*

Kind words create a very different home environment to critical and sometimes cruel observations. It's what we do if we respect others.

e) Discipline – we spend a whole chapter on this area later, but for the moment let's be clear that if we're not guiding and correcting the behaviours of our children we certainly won't be respecting them. Bad behaviour shows as much disrespect for ourselves as for others, so if we do possess a special regard for our children we will help them to understand these consequences and support them as they work out what is and isn't acceptable.

Rude children aren't easily accepted and perversely their reaction to rejection is often just to get worse! We are letting them down badly if this happens.

f) Respecting personal space and boundaries – this is something that gets particularly important the older your children get. You may think that their room is a pit but would you want your child to root about your room even if they were trying to tidy it? You would expect to be asked permission and why would that be any different for your children?

There seems to be a direct correlation between age and the shutting of bedroom doors. However, doors are shut for a reason and even though we may be overcome by curiosity and even suspicions of why that should be, we should still knock before entering even though we own the place!

There may be genuine exceptions of course when we are particularly concerned, perhaps for their safety, but back to the default setting analogy. I think trust rather than suspicion should be Dad's default setting because Dad always trusts.

And finally...

William of Wykeham coined the famous motto 'Manners maketh man' back in the 14th century. It's a timeless observation built on the foundation of respect, of honouring others.

That's how a Dad behaves because the essence of Dad is a man who respects his partner and his children. He is a gentle man. A Dad who isn't rude.

What will change?

1. If you don't do so already make meal times special times for communicating as a family. You will see the benefit even if it's just once or twice a week sitting down together around a table with no other distractions other than each other.

2. Begin each morning with a genuine 'good morning' and a smile for your children – don't worry if you need to rehearse this in the mirror first!

3. Why not have a go (with your children) of coming up with a set of 'Respect Rules' for your home? The 2003 England rugby union team did something similar and look what they achieved as a group!

Dad isn't self-seeking

Who is the number one in your life? Is it your partner, your children (or even just one of them) or is it you?

We will have all come across people whose core value appears to be 'Me'; the survival, advancement and ultimate success of 'Me'. These are selfish people: people who see the world with 'Me' at the centre of it; people who evaluate, both consciously and unconsciously, anything that comes along in terms of the impact on 'Me'.

And let's be honest, there is something of that in all of us. The drive for self-preservation is very strong particularly where physical pain is involved. But even beyond this most basic of instincts, there will be times – many times – when the first person who slips into our minds is 'Me'.

So the default position is probably that we are self-seeking by nature, but something happens when we become Dads and even before that when we choose our life partner. Someone else suddenly joins us and jostles for space at the centre of our world and in the case of a child they do it noisily and without any qualms. There can be little doubt in my view that the most selfish human beings on earth are babies with the core motivation of their little lives being the comfort of their bellies and bottoms!

But we respond to these needs driven by another very powerful instinct and emotion – love. Not just for another but for one that is OURS. At this point we gladly sacrifice our own needs and wants for the wonderful little miracle in front of us, and in fact the nearest thing I can compare the feelings I had on the birth of my first child was to being in love. I danced down the middle of the road the evening she was born with sheer joy (even though emboldened by a couple of glasses of champagne)! My wife had been the only person in my life who had been able to release that depth of emotion before.

However, as time moves on things become more challenging and 'Me' starts to loom large again as the real impact of parenthood starts to unfold, and if the truth is told, they never stop unfolding! We wouldn't dream of calling our little baby selfish however much he or she may scream and keep us awake at all hours, but phrases like 'You selfish little madam' do get uttered from time to time by a frustrated parent whose life seems to revolve around a perpetually ungrateful 'princess'!

So what about Dad? What does it mean for us NOT to be self-seeking? Well first here are some thoughts about what it DOESN'T mean:

a) It doesn't mean there is no room for Dad as No 1.

We all need space from time to time and there's nothing wrong about occasionally setting aside the sacrifices of time and money you are making for your children to look after yourself. For a start you need to go to work but you also need times of recreation through whatever you enjoy, be that with others or just by yourself. We all have different ways of recharging our batteries but we are all the same in that all of our batteries can run flat and that's no good for anyone least of all our children. A worn-out Dad is a crabby and short-tempered Dad whose perspective has deserted him somewhere along a long and weary road.

There is something else here as well. Dads probably find it easier to draw the line and find space than Mums so we probably need to keep an eye out for this and ensure that our partner also makes time for herself; that may be by herself or with friends but also may be at the same time as you. I've already mentioned 'date nights' earlier in this book; the idea may still sound corny to you but for many it is an oasis for each other as we come to terms with the challenges of parenthood. It is incredibly important for children to know and see how their parents love each other, but it's difficult for any relationship to grow without quality time together.

b) It doesn't mean our child is always No 1

If there's anything worse than a selfish Dad it's probably a selfish child! It's a thin line between the selflessness of Dad and the indulgence of little Johnnie or Jenny. A key part of Dad being self-seeking is to help their child to understand what it means NOT to be self-seeking.

It's up to you and your partner to teach them that love is primarily about what you can give rather than what you can get and paradoxically that selflessness is what's best for 'Me' in the long run. That's not why we put others first but that's what happens.

Sometimes it's right to say 'No' to your child and we'll come onto boundaries in 'Dad doesn't delight in evil but rejoices with the truth'. A selfless Dad isn't a doormat but a strong and in control Dad choosing to live his life looking out for others rather than looking in to himself.

So what DOES it mean NOT to be self-seeking? You may spot some repetition here because a Dad who isn't self-seeking will demonstrate many or all of the other 'Dad is...' behaviours:

- **Dad will show humility** – you'll know what you're good at but won't take up valuable airspace at home telling your family about it. You make room for your children to talk about what they have done and not make unhelpful comparisons with what you achieved at their age. Your children will rarely think you're disappointed in them.

- **Dad will make quality time for his children** – children will know that Dad has other things on his plate apart from them but will know that Dad makes special times for them in spite of the pressures. They will be OK even with your quite long absences through work if they know they have these times when you will be there for them, 100% there for them.

- **Dad will go without but your children won't know** – I don't think we should ever make our children feel guilt for anything we have given up to provide for them. If they squander what we give them that's their loss and not ours; piling guilt for what they have done to us on top of the guilt they will already feel won't help them at all. Sometimes they may never know what we have sacrificed for them but is that important? Being praised for sacrifice is like polishing silver with a scourer. It's not appropriate and spoils what you have done.

- **Dad will talk positively and honestly about others** – an 'other seeking' Dad will talk about and consider the needs of others in a way that benefits others. They will want the best for others and will be quick to recognise and be happy in the achievements of others. They will commend rather than condemn in conversation and particularly when it's about their own children.

- **Dad will look to support the passions of his children rather than get them to follow his** – we may think we know what's best for our children but often this has been polluted by what we think was best for us and even what our own parents thought was best for us.

You may have played rugby to a senior level but your son may want to dance! You may have a mainstream degree from a leading university but your daughter may want to style hair. By all means let's help our children to make the most of their talents, but let's open our minds to how many different ways there are to do that.

- **Dad will take on board criticism and say sorry** – I know we've already covered this but a Dad who is prepared to admit that he's not always right will be loved by his children (and his partner). If you want to splice two ropes together they first need to be unpicked and we can all do with a bit of 'unpicking' from time to time as we grow in relationship with our children.

Don't take yourself too seriously. Admitting to frailties and even failure makes us so much more accessible to our children and teaches them about getting the right perspective about themselves, and to be comfortable in their own skin.

- **Dad will do the right thing for his children even when it's not convenient for him** – they will know that if it's really important that Dad will drop any and everything he is doing for them.

- **Dad will be kind and generous** – sometimes with money, sometimes with time, sometimes with treats, sometimes with surprises but always with love and the genuine best interests of his children at heart.

And finally...

A Dad who isn't self-seeking knows the truth of the saying, 'It is more blessed to give than to receive', or said in another way 'You're far happier giving than getting'.

Your children can see that you know that from the way you behave. They will be proud that they have an outwardly focused Dad who thinks in terms of 'He, She and They' far more than Me. And your example will help them to grow into considerate, courteous young adults who spend as much if not more time thinking about others as themselves.

What will change?

1. How are you doing with any adjustments you made to your diary to ensure you get quality time with your children? Are the rocks in place yet?

2. Have a look at your children's interest and activities – are these about them or about you?

3. Is there anything you've done that you should have said sorry to your children about and not done so? Why not lay any pride or self-justification aside and simply sit down with them and tell them how sorry we are.

4. Are you getting enough space to recharge? How about Mum as well? Make sure you get these times in the diary – they're another 'Rock' example.

Dad isn't easily angered

When my eldest daughter was about two years old she wasn't the best at eating her dinner. I was a young Dad, hassled from a busy day at work trying to do my best to encourage her to eat her plate of baked beans which was just about the only thing we could get down her at that stage.

And then it happened. I just snapped, picked up the plate and tipped the now cold beans over her head before storming out of the room. Now I said that I was hassled but what about my wife who was now at 'try to encourage Gemma to eat' meal number 21 for the week as well as looking after a recently arrived baby sister? She was the one who had to literally pick up the pieces – cold sticky and congealing baked bean pieces not only off my screaming daughter's face, but also the floor and those little crevices in high chairs that somebody, someday will realise need to be designed out!

This all may sound funny but it certainly wasn't for my wife or daughter at the time, the same daughter, you may recall, who had mentioned me going to every sports day in her pre-university 'thank you' scrapbook. Yes, and you've guessed it, what became known as the 'baked bean incident' appeared in there as well just to ensure a balanced view of my parenting skills!

We're all susceptible to anger from time to time not only as Dads but also as men in our everyday lives. It's not nice being on the end of someone's anger and I always find that when I lose my temper it doesn't feel very nice for me either.

There are some really good reasons why it's not a good idea to be easily angered with our children:

- Quite simply it can frighten them.
- If it happens 'out of the blue' the unpredictability of our reaction can be as worrying as the anger itself.
- When you're angry you are normally at the limit of your self-control and possibly out of control, and that's when things are said or done that we regret, and are not always easily forgotten.
- All of this, if it happens enough, can destroy the trust and respect of your children for you.

At some stage as a Dad we will probably 'lose it' but when we do the key thing is to get back in control quickly and very probably apologise for our actions. It is said that 'revenge is a dish best served cold' but anger is almost certainly best served cold!

But is anger always wrong? Out of control anger probably is but our definition says that Dad isn't EASILY angered. Occasional and justified anger properly channelled can have a powerful and positive impact on our children.

Occasional – because frequent outbursts lose their impact and are probably mostly uncontrolled and impulsive anyway. There's quite a weight of research about nowadays that suggests that children tend to respond and flourish more when the balance of feedback is positive rather than negative.

Justified – because we need to pick what's really important to be angry about. Remember that Dad is patient and will pick the right battles to fight in the context of the longer term. We should be up in the helicopter and the time it takes for us to descend in times of crisis should give us enough space to let our internal anger temperature drop to a manageable level.

How often is occasional and how serious is justified?

Sorry, I have no quick and easy answers to those questions. What I do know is that as you try to find the right balance you will make mistakes, but that doesn't mean you've failed. You're just spending some time working out first of all how to get out of the long grass and then how to avoid getting into it again.

Here are a few things I think I've been justified to get angry about:

1. Lying or covering up the truth.
2. Persistent lack of effort in school.
3. Physical harming of another.
4. Pre-meditated unkindness.
5. Persistent disobedience.

That's certainly not a particularly comprehensive list but may help in that it DOESN'T include a lot of the silly little things that we DO get so angry about like knocking over a glass of water, or recording over the last episode of our favourite TV drama, or missing an open goal in the school football match.

I've just popped down for a cup of tea with my wife and she said something interesting about anger: 'Do you think it's ever justified to be angry with a **person**?'

Come to think of it the short 'justified anger list' above is all about behaviours, so perhaps there is something here about focusing the articulation of our anger on the behaviour rather than the person? So 'that was a thoughtless thing to do' is probably more helpful than 'you're stupid'!

If too much anger isn't helpful how do we avoid being easily angered? 'Counting to ten' is a possible last resort but it's much better to head off the pressures well before we get to that point. We all have our own set of 'buttons' that when pressed can spark off a disproportionate reaction, but these are probably in the list for a lot of us:

- **Tiredness** – it lowers our defences and tolerance levels particularly when combined with alcohol, hunger or just feeling under the weather. Looking after our physical well-being will probably head off a lot of our angry outbursts.

- **Not dealing with past misdemeanours** – there's little point in suppressing annoyance or hurt as the pressure will build and build until it finally erupts in anger. 'Don't let the sun go down on your anger' is good advice as it's usually best to deal with small niggles as soon as we can rather than let them mutate into an unreasonable red-eyed monster! Dad keeps no record of wrongs.

- **Unreasonable expectations** – the higher we set the bar on behaviour the more our children will knock it down. Perhaps there are areas where it can be set a little lower to give your children more space and to avoid unnecessary flashpoints?

- **Outside pressures** – often the things that we're really riled about have nothing to do with the children. A bad day at work or even a disagreement with our partner will leave us exposed to even the smallest provocation. It's all too easy to let some of the pressure off by picking on our children rather than dealing with what is really annoying us.

I find that simple things like not working on the train or including a short walk in my journey home help me to unwind after a busy day BEFORE I walk through the door. Different things work for different people but do try to find your way and stick to it.

And finally...

If you find that your anger is becoming too frequent and lacks justification you probably do need to seek help. This may start by talking things through with your partner or a trusted friend but sometimes a visit to the GP may be advisable as a useful 'best next step' in helping to manage your anger more effectively.

All the time you put this off it will be your children that get caught in the crossfire because it's at home where you will behave how you really feel. Our children have an incredible capacity to forgive but let's not let our avoidance of a real problem test that tolerance beyond its limits.

What will change?

1. Think of the last time you got angry and do some self-analysis, perhaps with your partner acting as an honest sounding board.

    -   What was I angry about?
    -   Was my reaction justified and proportionate?
    -   Were there any other pressures at play and what can I do to manage these better in future?
    -   Do I need to do any explaining or apologise to my children?
    -   If my reaction was justified and proportionate is there any follow-up to do with my child? The next chapter may help with this one.

2. Make a list of the things that help you to unwind the best. Share these with your partner and get a selection of them in the diary on a regular basis.

Dad keeps no record of wrongs

The one thing you can be certain that you will need in any relationship and particularly with your children is forgiveness. Your child will do something wrong and, just as likely, you will do something wrong. Either way, if the damage isn't quickly repaired the wounds harden and scar and create ongoing problems, and sometimes even seemingly irreconcilable separation.

Unforgiveness is like the bad apple in the fruit bowl or the tiny bacteria left in a cleaned wound; the rottenness and disease can spread to infect far beyond its original self. We often call this bitterness and bitterness consumes us and saps our joy even when our hurt or indignation at the way we have been wronged is justified. And this can happen even when the other person is oblivious to the hurt they have caused another.

Lewis B Smedes was onto something when he said: 'To forgive is to set a prisoner free and discover that the prisoner was you.'

Forgiveness is what repairs relationships in a way that not only heals them, but also makes them stronger.

And it certainly cannot be considered a sign of weakness when a man like Mahatma Gandhi observes that: 'The weak can never forgive. Forgiveness is the attribute of the strong.'

So how many times can you forgive your own child? Is there anything you cannot or should not forgive? These are interesting and in some instances relevant, critical and even urgent questions but remember what I said in 'Dad isn't proud'; it's often the small everyday misdemeanours that can grow out of all proportion so that's what I'll focus on here. We'll touch again on the more extreme circumstances in 'Dad never fails'.

So what do we understand by forgiveness? Do you remember what we talked about in the last chapter and my wife's challenge about is it ever right to be angry with a person? Well one way of looking at forgiveness is by recognising that our relationship with our children is more important than anything they may have done. In other words:

FORGIVENESS MEANS LETTING GO OF WHAT HAS BEEN DONE BY OUR CHILD SO WE ARE ABLE TO TAKE HOLD OF OUR CHILD.

There are two laws generally at work here that we will need to be aware of and work with:

- The bigger the offence, the harder it usually is to let go of it.
- The longer we hold onto the offence, however small it may be, the harder it is to let go.

These laws will operate quite happily unless we DECIDE to do something about it and then TAKE ACTION to express what we have decided. If we don't do that, even if we say we forgive our child, the offence will still lurk on a list to be brought out at any time they may transgress again in the future.

Have you thought whilst reading this book as to why our 'Dad Definition' expresses so much of its content in terms of what Dad isn't? Perhaps it's because the writer of the original love definition felt that we would learn more by looking at the diametrically opposed expression.

But with forgiveness we revert to a positive definition of what Dad DOES do and that means he keeps **NO RECORD** OF WRONGS. So the big and conscious decision we need to make when we forgive is not to keep a list of past indiscretions; we have to work out how we can both forgive **AND** forget.

Why is keeping no record of wrongs so important and what is the rationale for taking this approach with our children in particular? Essentially I think it's about shaping the way a child sees and values themselves and critically the reason why they are loved by you.

Remember what my young son said about why he thought I loved him: 'Because you're my Dad.' You don't need to be advanced in years to have wisdom and understanding!

That's why we love our children isn't it? Because we're their Dad or Mum and NOT because they're a 'good boy or girl'. Their behaviour has nothing to do with our love for them but continually bringing up past misdemeanours will make them think just the opposite.

How does this work in practice? I've tried hard not to make this a 'How to be a Dad' manual because my own experience is that what's more important is to get my head around the principles and then work out the practice in a way that is tailored to my own children as individuals.

However, I do still find practical ideas useful in framing how I respond. I've also learned a lot from observing what has and hasn't worked with friends as well as what Anna and I have tried. So here are a few:

- First of all an easy one – or is it because it takes time to do well? Let your child know your displeasure. Be specific about what they have done wrong and what the consequence of their action has been. Tell them how it has made you or whoever they have wronged feel. This not only helps them to understand what they have to change but also encourages them to say sorry at a deeper level. It's also much easier to forgive a truly sorry child.

- Try talking them through what alternative (and better) actions they could have taken. What would have been the outcome of making that choice? Understanding 'what good looks like' is nearly always a lot more useful than being told what you've got wrong.

- Focus on their behaviour rather than upon them. Your child needs to be responsible for what they do but just because they fail doesn't mean to say that they are a failure.

- We'll come to this in more detail in the next chapter but there may well be existing consequences of their behaviour and this may need to be repaired by them or a punishment to be taken. Forgiveness doesn't mean a complete avoidance of consequences.

- However, your forgiveness should be unconditional – no strings attached. You should forgive before exercising the punishment because as we noted above, your love for your child is dependent on who they are and not on how they behave.

Punishment is about reparation for the past and a deterrent for the future, but your forgiveness is a reminder to your child that their behaviour hasn't changed the way you love them.

- Instead of keeping a mental list of past transgressions write down a list of the good and positive things they have done. Let them look at it themselves as what they see will make them feel far better than when they messed up.

- Before you start the talking, think about the environment. Try to have the conversation one to one without interruption and sitting down so you can look at each other. Eye contact is as important for making sure forgiveness has sunk in as it is for communicating displeasure at the errant behaviour.

- Physical contact helps with the forgiveness process – in other words give each other a hug! Even though you may initially resist inside this type of contact just seems to squeeze away the tension and resistance. You can almost feel the relationship mending going on as the warming peace of reconciliation moved through you. That may seem a bit too lyrical but it's what it really does feel like.

- Use the words 'I forgive you'. Even consider saying 'All forgotten'. Often you need to say something before the heart follows.

And some things to avoid:

- Delaying the communication of your forgiveness. Withholding forgiveness should never be part of the punishment. 'Don't let the sun go down on your anger' is real practical advice. Try to sort things out on the same day, both the saying sorry and the 'I forgive you'.

- Letting past behaviours shape the way you see the present too much. Positive past experiences tend to build trust in our children while the opposite can makes us suspicious of even the most genuine actions.

- However, we do need to give time and room for our children to change without the shadow of the past hanging over them. We will all remember the 'Naughty Boy' or 'Little Madam' at school, but too often that reputation hangs around long after any such label may have been justified. If we saw them in the street today it would probably still be the image that immediately springs to mind.

- In the same way we should be careful of a positive past track record blinding us to an emerging problem. How many times do we hear the words 'I never saw it coming'.

- Be careful about bringing up past bad behaviour even if in retrospect it was rather funny. Beware of the cheap laugh particularly amongst friends. There are some things that should be kept quiet because there should be no record of them happening in the first place!

Whether you know who Bernard Meltzer is or not (a well-known and respected host of a US radio advice call-in show, *"What's Your Problem?"* his words hold a strong ring of truth:

WHEN YOU FORGIVE YOU IN NO WAY CHANGE THE PAST BUT YOU SURE DO CHANGE THE FUTURE.

The future of a child you love because of who they are and for whom, in spite of the past, you will always have high hopes because 'Dad always hopes'.

And finally...

Remember the quote at the start of the chapter about who is the real prisoner? Demonstrating forgiveness to your children will in turn help them forgive those who have hurt them in some way. Children who watch a positive Dad letting go of an offence to keep hold of a relationship will more easily do the same themselves.

It is within our power not to leave them with an inheritance of bitterness, resentment and regret.

What will change?

1. Can you still remember things your children have done wrong in the past and do you still bring these up or let them influence the way you see your child? If the answer is 'Yes' why not try writing them down on a piece of paper and then burning or shredding it.

2. Give your child a hug and tell them you love them. Do it often and at any time so they don't associate it with the way they behave.

3. Is there anything unresolved with your partner? If your children see the symptoms of unforgiveness – bitterness, resentment and bringing up the past in arguments – there is a real danger that they will assume you both feel the same way about them. Try your very best to sort out anything that's unresolved between you.

4. Make sure that the last memory your child has before they go to sleep is a positive one. Even if there are still consequences or a punishment to endure they should know that their Dad and Mum forgives them.

Dad doesn't delight in evil but rejoices with the truth

You may have heard the phrase 'Feedback is the food of champions' and I don't know about you but I see my children as 'champions'!

Feedback can come in many forms but basically there are two types. Some call these negative and positive but I prefer correcting and reinforcing and as far as our children are concerned these take the form of 'discipline' and 'praise'.

Let's take a step back for a moment and ask a really important question – perhaps we should have done that before but now it's especially relevant: **What is the objective of parenting?**

We will all have our particular views on this but part of how we answer would very probably include something about preparing them for adulthood. We want to see well-adjusted, happy, secure and confident individuals who are able to find their own place in the world as they embrace the particular opportunities that come their way. We want them to be able to relate to others the best they can, to work hard and well, and if they are blessed with a life partner and children to pass on what they have learned from us – and more.

So for me it's to raise children that will make a positive difference in their families, friendship groups, work place and even beyond.

And as we work towards this objective we have two tools we just cannot do without, helping them to enjoy the present as a child whilst shaping them for their future as an adult –

discipline and praise – tools that will teach them how to make good choices themselves.

Discipline – Dad doesn't delight in evil

There are few areas of parental practice that can cause a falling out between friends and even partners than the way we discipline our children. But we will probably all agree that there are few parental activities that are more important than setting (and later negotiating) boundaries, determining consequences and seeing them through so that our children learn the practice of self-discipline.

THE PURPOSE OF DISCIPLINE MUST BE TO TEACH SELF-DISCIPLINE BECAUSE WE WON'T ALWAYS BE THERE.

A disciplined child isn't a repressed child but one with a self-awareness and self-control that enables them to make the best of their relationships, abilities and learning through their formative years and right into adulthood.

Sorry but once again the next bit could seem that I'm getting into 'Dad Instruction Manual' mode. I don't mean it to be like that but what I'm seeking to do is to throw out some suggestions that will help you to think. It's certainly not a list of 'Golden Rules' for you to follow slavishly, and if you decide to do the opposite it's not for me to disagree on what's right for YOUR child.

a) Set clear boundaries – 'make sure you're not too late' is open to and will be subject to a wide range of differing interpretations by your teenager. 'Make sure you're home by 11 and let us know if this becomes a problem' is clear and unequivocal.

b) Set boundaries at a sensible level remembering to take the helicopter view because Dad is patient. Try to keep them simple, clear and to a minimum.

c) Explain why you have set the boundaries where you have. There is a place for the 'because I said so' school of reasoning but as your children get older part of building the skill of self-discipline is to understand how to set a boundary in the first place. For some this starts much earlier than others, so be sensitive to the particular personality of your child.

d) Be clear in outlining the consequences of crossing the boundaries that you set. *Supernanny* has immortalised the concept of the 'naughty step' and I have seen my own children use this type of approach successfully with some of my grandchildren. In fact, they tell me it's called the 'time-out step' now!

The range of consequences can be as wide as the list of naughty behaviours but whatever one you choose try to make sure that it's proportionate to the 'crime' and that it's possible to carry it out. Consequences made up in the heat of the moment tend to fail both of these criteria so it's a good idea for Mum and Dad to prepare and agree a menu of options in advance.

Work out what works for each particular child as they are all different and motivated in different ways. For some all they need is a look whilst for others it's 30 minutes in their bedroom.

e) Follow through on the consequences. This does require discipline and concentration from us. Lack of follow-through on consequences often happens not because we're too soft but because we get distracted by something else or we're just really tired.

f) Talking about choices can be helpful; most times we have a choice as to what we do in a particular situation and understanding how to evaluate options can teach our children how they can take control of their lives and destinies. Bad consequences come from poor choices and there is normally a better way that leads to a positive outcome and even praise.

g) Try to avoid disciplining your child in public even if the behaviour happens in front of others as it invariably will. If action needs to be taken then try removing them from the situation – perhaps take them to another room – as the very act not only introduces a delay that helps you to 'cool down' before administering any punishment, but also keeps their dignity intact.

Also do your best to remember that the discipline is for the benefit of your child and not the people you are with. Is it a good idea to be overly influenced by what others think?

In fact it nearly always helps to have a 'cool down' delay before administering correction. That's why consequences like the 'naughty step' or 'time outs' are so useful. They remove both us and our children from the flashpoint until we are in a more stable state of mind to decide how best to proceed. Remember that 'Dad isn't easily angered'.

h) Be consistent in the boundaries and consequences you set both as individual parents but particularly as a team. If there is any variation between parents our children will pick it up and exploit it as much as they can. I'm convinced our children had consulted with each other at some length and agreed strategies for whether to approach Mum or Dad in any particular situation!

But seriously, predictability is important for security and without it the result can be an insecure child who grows into an unpredictable adult.

i) This one is connected to the last. Don't undermine the discipline of your partner. If you disagree, wait until the children aren't about and then talk it through until you reach agreement. If the result of this is that one of you has over-reacted (very probably Dad) make sure you square this off with your child and apologise if you need to.

j) Once the punishment is done with, take time to talk through what happened with your child. Perhaps ask them to explain why they think they have been punished. The lesson may not stick the first time but with consistency and persistency they will learn to make better choices for themselves.

Praise – Dad rejoices with the truth

Letting your children know how you feel when they get things right is every bit as powerful as when they get things wrong. When it comes to developing your children as people, discipline and praise are really both sides of the same coin.

And that means that many of the suggestions we have covered in relation to discipline apply just as much to praise. For example, spontaneous and unstructured praise has its place but can sometimes short-change our child of the full benefits of planned recognition. However, there are also some important differences to note as we work through another list of suggestions, this time about praise:

a) Be careful about over-using praise as a planned and communicated reward for achieving a particular benchmark. The reason I say this is that a child can very easily base their identity and worth on what they achieve rather than who they are.

b) This could be contentious but I think that elements of the so-called 'high performance culture' approach that's so prevalent in business can be as dangerous as they are untruthful. Phrases like 'You're as good as your last set of results' are absolute rubbish! You don't suddenly become a bad employee or manager because of one set of results, that's nonsense!

Paying a teenager £100 for every grade A at GCSE doesn't only become very expensive but could teach the child that personal achievement in life is defined purely by a narrow definition of results. What if you have a very bright child and another of average academic ability? Is one more deserving of praise and reward than the other? Is it fair and just that one gets rich after exams and not the other? Do you pay one for As and the other for passes?

We also need to be careful about conditioning our children to expect praise if they do a particular thing. We all know that praise can be both inconsistent and in short supply out in the world and just because no one says anything doesn't mean to say we're not doing the right things. We need to help our children develop and have confidence in their own internal barometer of what is good and what is right.

c) Be generous, frequent and wide-ranging in your praise. Work hard at 'catching them doing something right' – it's not only more enjoyable than 'catching them doing something wrong' but probably much more effective.

That doesn't mean to say that punishment doesn't have its place in providing correction but that we need to think carefully about the balance between praise and discipline. They are both different sides of the same coin and understanding the benefits of positive consequences can be just as powerful as avoiding punishment.

When my son was at school he played in the same football side as the son of an ex-England footballer and accomplished coach. The Dad used to come to all the matches and as you would expect was reasonably vocal from the touchlines. However, all I ever heard coming from his mouth was positive encouragement: 'Well done'; 'Great'; 'Next time, son' etc. I commented on this after one game and remember him saying that in his experience it wasn't just boys who respond best to praise but also Premiership footballers!

d) However, in your search for 'things done right' ensure that your praise is genuine. If your child has messed up something because of their lack of care or application they know that and trying to say 'well done' to them just isn't truthful. By all means find positives to build on, but they need to recognise and address the truth of what they have done.

e) Be specific with your praise – 'Well done that was very kind' is a good start but why was it kind? 'The way you looked after your younger brother this afternoon by playing the games he wanted to play rather than what you wanted to do was really kind'. That gives specifics that can help to build your child's understanding of what was kind behaviour.

f) Praise behaviours more than results as very rarely do the ends justify the means. Is a person defined and remembered more by their character or by what they achieve?

g) Surprise them with your praise and don't be afraid to show genuine delight. I know running onto the pitch at the end of a game to embrace your son or daughter can embarrass them, but they love seeing the broad grin of pride on your face more than almost anything. My son still remembers and laughs about his Mum shouting out 'I gave birth to him,' as he scored the winning penalty in a cup final shoot-out!

h) Dad keeps no record of wrongs but there's every reason to keep a record of achievements for your children. I would also suggest that they keep this for themselves and that you work on it together – their 'Me File'. Make sure the definition of 'achievement' is drawn widely and includes things like letters and emails of thanks, or pictures of them looking stunning in their ball gown as well as 50m swimming certificates and the like.

i) I know I've said that your praise should have integrity but I think there's a place to push the boundaries on this a bit with your teenage daughters and particularly when it comes to their appearance. Your child is only too aware of their spots and greasy hair but still need to hear 'you look beautiful' from their Dad. And actually that IS your honest assessment as you look at your little princess with a heart bursting with joy and pride.

Don't forget your boys either – if they've had a stinker on the football pitch they know it and don't need their Dad on their case in the car on the way home. But they still want to hear you 'big-up' the good things they did!

j) I've heard some advice that you discipline your child in private but praise them in public. We've already covered this in 'Dad doesn't boast' but I would counsel against too much public praise remembering that there are few more powerful encouragements than Dad saying well done privately, one to one, with your attention 100% on them.

k) Be careful what behaviour you reinforce by your reactions. Children will perform to an audience; some naughty behaviours in a two year old may be funny, but if you correct the child and still draw the attention of your friends to the comedy you will be sending mixed messages. A child who learns to respond in this way can all too soon find the label of 'cute' converting to 'brat'.

A short and helpful interlude...

I've just popped downstairs for a break and once again came back up with some inspiration, this time from one of my daughters. I chatted through what I've been writing in this chapter and she came up with a really good example of how discipline becomes self-discipline.

The school her two girls attend has a chart on the wall with a rainbow in the middle and above the rainbow a sun and then some stars. Below the rainbow is a cloud and then underneath that a rain cloud so you've probably already worked out how this works.

Everyone starts with their name-tag on the rainbow and if they do something particularly good they advance to the sun. If they do something good again they get up to the stars and are given a star sticker to wear. Conversely, if they misbehave they move down to the cloud, and if they continue in that way they end up on the rain cloud, and finally with a visit to the head teacher!

Now I'm sure we will all have views on the merits or otherwise of this approach, but the interesting thing is that my granddaughters have recreated this chart on the wall of their bedroom at home. The other day my daughter went into the room and found the eldest had her name on the cloud. She asked why and her daughter explained that because she had done something naughty earlier that day she had decided the cloud is where she should be at the moment. How about that for self-awareness and self-discipline!

My daughter also noticed that 'Mum' and 'Dad' name-tags had appeared on this home-grown version of the chart and that Dad was on the rain cloud. 'That's because he farted this morning,' explained the other granddaughter!

Some final thoughts on discipline and praise

I don't know whether you've noticed this already but I've found it striking how the various other elements of the 'Dad is' definition become relevant as we work out how to discipline and praise our children:

- **Dad is patient** – remembering to take the long-term view when deciding how to correct or encourage a child.
- **Dad is kind** – our children knowing that behind the discipline is a Dad's heart that wants the best for his child.
- **Dad doesn't envy** – we are genuinely happy for the success of our children and are grateful for the personality, skills and relationships that they have in their own right and not in comparison with others.
- **Dad doesn't boast** – we're careful about publicly praising our child for our as well as their benefit.
- **Dad isn't proud** – we're proud of our children but we're not too proud ourselves to admit where we get our discipline wrong and say sorry.
- **Dad doesn't dishonour others** – respect for our child is at the heart of our discipline. They know the positive regard we hold them in whatever they think of the relevance of the boundary we have put in place.
- **Dad isn't self-seeking** – we will make time to celebrate the success of our children and to properly think through the approach to their discipline with our partner.
- **Dad isn't easily angered** – anger and discipline make a dangerous cocktail so we adopt strategies to ensure we administer punishment in a considered way rather than in the heat of the moment.
- **Dad keeps no record of wrongs** – Dad will discipline but won't keep bringing up past mistakes. We look to catch our

children doing something right rather than continuing to focus on shortcomings.

And finally...

The exercise of discipline and praise is where 'the rubber really hits the road' when it comes to being a Dad. There are no easy answers or formulas but if a child experiences correction or positive reinforcement from a kind and patient Dad, there are few influences that will be more important as part of their development into a champion adult who makes a real difference in their world.

What will change?

1. Try writing down a list of consequences with your partner that you can draw on in a pressurised disciplining situation.

2. Think of a time recently when you over-reacted. Talk to your child about what happened and say sorry.

3. Try playing this version of the 'game of consequences' with your partner, children and friends. Each of you write your name at the bottom of a piece of paper and then pass it on. When you get the next sheet write something positive down about the person whose name is on the paper. Do this at the top of the paper and then fold it over so your comments are hidden.

Pass it on to the next person and then do the same again with the next sheet you have. Continue with this process until the paper with your name on it gets back to you. There will be a complete list of encouraging comments in your hand now but don't read it just yet. Pass it on to the next person and then each person in turn reads out the comments to the whole group as well as to you.

It might seem embarrassing but there is real power in hearing as well as reading nice things that have been said about you. You will also hear people chipping in with support and approval. Encourage your children to keep the piece of paper in a safe place and to look at it if they ever feel down.

Dad always protects

Strong words don't leave much room for movement and the next four chapters are about a couple of these 'totally committed' words – 'Always' and 'Never'. Dad ALWAYS protects, ALWAYS hopes, ALWAYS trusts, ALWAYS perseveres.

Please don't put the book down at this point! We all know that being a Dad is challenging but remember what we said earlier – YOU'RE NOT THE ONLY ONE. Others are travelling the same journey and probably getting lost or falling over at the same points. We can be there to encourage and help each other as well as our children in much the same way that marathon runners help each other though 'the wall' even if it's just by knowing the other is there.

So who wouldn't jump to protect their own child; probably do anything to protect their own child? There are some extreme occasions where this may not be the case but most of the time our 'default setting' is turned firmly to 'protect' mode.

But what does this mean in practice? Is it about wrapping them up in cotton wool so the world cannot possibly harm them? Probably not, particularly when we remember what the objective of parenthood is – to prepare them for the time when they are adults making their own way and difference. But sometimes it is, particularly when they are very young or get themselves into serious trouble.

Most of the time though I see it in terms of what the army calls 'keeping your back covered'. The soldier is taking personal responsibility and personal risks but his colleague is keeping a look out for unforeseen danger, and will even intervene if there's not enough time to warn of the impending danger.

The 'helicopter view' analogy also works well in this context as we have the experience and detachment to be able to see a lot of what's coming and to warn and guide our children. And occasionally we need to land to give support or remove them from serious danger when they either cannot or won't hear us!

We need to be careful about doing this too often because sometimes they need to experience the consequence of their choices to learn, but all the time we are watching their back to ensure the danger to them or others isn't too great.

IT'S ALL VERY WELL GIVING THEM ENOUGH ROPE TO HANG THEMSELVES BUT DO REMEMBER TO KEEP HOLD OF THE OTHER END OF THE ROPE!

Being able to see and think ahead enables us to help our children to learn an important life lesson – to avoid unnecessary trouble by putting yourself out of harm's way.

Sometimes it's really hard to get this message across; for example, we were always nervous about our children watching adult rated movies when they were young – horror, violence, explicit sex, that sort of thing. Sleepover parties in the early teens are a nightmare in this context – do you forbid them to go and risk them being ostracised by a group of friends as well as missing out on a fun time together to build relationships?

There's no easy answer but it's normally helpful to talk to the parents of the hosting child to see what guidelines they will be putting in place for the event. Some parents see nothing wrong in a group of 12 year olds watching a horror film, but most will and make efforts to avoid this happening particularly if another parent has expressed concern. If they laugh it off personally I wouldn't let my child go, and would then explain to them why. It's difficult though isn't it? But Dad always protects.

Have you or your child ever been bullied? That's another difficult area but there is a myth we need to dispel here – and it looms large in your child's mind – that your intervention will only make things worse. My experience is that it doesn't at all, and if the bullying is happening at school most establishments now have a very clear and effective bullying policy. Dad should absolutely do all he can to protect his child in these circumstances enlisting the help of others, like teachers, who are there when he's not there.

Cyber-bullying is more difficult and this pulls in the whole area of **how to protect your child from harm on the internet**. You could write a whole book on this and the problem is becoming more and more difficult to control as devices to access the content become both more portable and affordable. This is an area where it's really easy either to be too relaxed or too strict, and often this is because we have been plain lazy in not giving enough time to understand the problem, and discuss with our partner and children how we deal with it.

This is serious. As parents it's absolutely vital that we take time to learn what the dangers are, what we can do to help make our children as safe as possible and then to implement the measures we decide to take.

We make a big thing of not letting our young teenagers out on the streets at night but let them wander around the whole world from their bedrooms.

Take time to Google something like 'Protecting your children online', but make sure you don't just end up 'putting up a fence' as the only means of protection. Most of us can find our way around, over or under a barrier if we really want to get to something on the other side. So we also need to work on reducing the strong motivation and pressures our children feel to explore beyond what we may consider to be safe online.

They are trying to be grown up and therefore treating them like a grown-up is probably a good course of action, working through the various choices they have when they start clicking, and what the consequences may be and regularly reviewing with them how things are going.

If you keep saying 'No' or insist on putting too many seemingly arbitrary boundaries in place don't be surprised when your children won't invite you as a 'Friend' on Facebook or the like. Work hard to educate yourself on how best to 'cover their backs' – there are plenty of resources and ideas out there and it's better to do something than nothing.

The list of areas where our children may need our protection is a long one – relationships, sex, alcohol and drugs immediately spring to the minds of parents.

Covering their backs in these areas isn't just about being there at the time, it's also about how we prepare for the potential 'conflict zone'.

I once had the privilege of hearing Rudolf Giuliani – the Mayor of New York at the time of 9/11 – speak on how the City of New York was able to respond so effectively to such an unprecedented disaster. He explained that although they didn't have a specific plan for airplanes being flown into skyscrapers they did have one for extreme weather conditions, or a flood in the metro or a major fire in Manhattan. These plans were close enough to enable them to respond quickly and effectively so he spoke passionately about the need for leaders to insist upon 'relentless preparation'. Isn't the safety and well-being of our children worthy of the same attention and diligence?

We may or may not get the imagined scenarios they get themselves into completely right, but at least we won't be making up our urgent response completely from scratch! Forewarned is forearmed. It's also much more productive to get your children involved at this stage and talk through the potential dangers than trying to do this when things have gone wrong. They will also probably have knowledge about dangers you've never even thought of!

Protecting your child from physical harm seems to be a 'no-brainer', but what about more subtle ways in which they can be damaged? For example, what is your first reaction when someone tells you something negative about what your child has done? Is it to believe it without question, or do you thank the person for the information without passing judgment before going back to discuss things with your child? We've probably all seen bosses at work who seem to assume the worst about their people, but it's really easy to do that with your children as well.

I'm not suggesting that you're blind to their faults although that can become a real danger. I'm just suggesting that you don't automatically jump to conclusions; your child's reputation is precious and if a parent doesn't have their back then who will?

The need to sometimes **protect your child from themselves** is a reality and can mean we need to be available to be where they need us at a moment's notice. As a Dad we want our children to have no hesitation in calling us if they are in really serious trouble. However, whether they will or not often depends on experience of our past reactions to them getting into trouble, particularly if it's through their own choices.

We build the trust our children need to cry out to us for help over many years; if we never have time for them or deal harshly with them they will hesitate to call us when they really need to.

You may think I'm a bit of a soft touch and overprotective, but I was always very happy to pick my daughters up from the local town at two in the morning. We encouraged them to work out how and when they would get home before these evenings started, and to have a back-up plan if things didn't work out.

And finally...

Is there any time or circumstance where we should give up trying to protect our children? Perhaps when they're 18 or 21 or when they leave home? I personally don't think it's that easy and you can find yourself covering their backs well into adulthood.

I don't see anything wrong with that; our role as a Dad will change with time but we will always be their Dad.

And Dad ALWAYS protects.

What will change?

1. Think about how you help your children prepare for potential danger. Don't do this in a rush but encourage them to sit down with you and articulate how they would respond to the unexpected (or even the expected). We all tend to be pretty good at 'Plan A' but few of us have a 'Plan B' when things go differently than planned.

   Examples include: Gap year travelling including staying in touch; a school skiing trip; a night out clubbing; sleepovers and parties; a first date. I'm sure you can think of a lot more!

2. Put an evening aside with your partner to research how to protect your child online, that way at least you'll identify what you don't know. Consider getting further guidance, perhaps through a local course, a book or just looking at resources online. You'll probably also find that you have friends who have already been down this path or know a lot more than you. Don't be afraid to ask them for help.

3. Tell your child why you want to protect them and get their views on what you have said. Children, even teenagers, will rarely respond negatively when they see their parents genuinely giving them time and care, and even though they may disagree with some of what you say at least you have had the conversation and something might stick, and you may even be pleasantly surprised how much thought they have put into their own safety!

Dad always trusts

Letting go of our children isn't a one-off event we go through when they leave home. It starts from a very early age and gradually prepares them and us for the big steps in independence that are to come.

As Dads we are meant to protect our children, to provide the safety net, but I don't think we're meant to cling onto them, at least not most of the time!

Sometimes we need to – like with a young child near a busy road or in a crowded shopping centre. You don't want to experience the excruciating worry of a lost child, or the near miss of an accident too often. However, where we are sure we can cover their backs we need to let go and trust them to try making the right choices for themselves.

We do it when we let go of them for the first time as they take their first staggering steps. We do it when we wave goodbye for the first time at the school gates. We do it when we leave them round a friend's house for their first 'play date'. Dads – we do it on our daughter's first date and that normally comes a lot sooner than we would prefer! We do it as they start their first job or go to university or start off on a gap year travelling adventure that seems to take in all the world's current political hotspots. And finally, we do it when they move into a place of their own or get married.

I believe that the way we start letting go and trusting our children in the small things – as early as we can – will determine their success at handling the far bigger steps that are to come.

A good friend of mine commented recently in the context of dieting that he has always embraced his changing stature and shape as he has grown older – in other words he enjoys his food and wine! It's much more important to embrace each different life stage we travel through with our children. It is important to gather memories but you don't drive with your eyes continually on the rearview mirror. The lessons of the past are what prepare us for the challenges and adventure of the future, so it's good for us as well as our children to embrace their growing independence rather than to hold on for too long.

But ALWAYS trusts? Are you sure? What if they abuse our trust, what then?

Once again I come back to the idea of 'default settings'. There will be times when our trust is sorely tested as promises are broken and bad choices made; our trust in our children may seem to be in pieces and require a substantial rebuild. However, most of the time that's not the case and our first reaction to events or situations – our default setting – should be positive and trusting.

If a child is trusted from an early age, and especially when they have messed up, they are likely to respond positively to our persistence in giving them responsibility. This isn't the same as indulgence or a lack of care, but rather to keep close through the failures so we can help them to learn the lessons and make the right choices next time.

A good place to start is the way we guide our toddlers how to behave when they're with their friends. If your child pushes other children over or bites or pinches you don't stop them from playing with others. You will discipline them and show clearly what is unacceptable but you demonstrate your trust in them by putting them back into the situation – sometimes many times over until they get the message. And you will praise them when they get things right.

The trust needed to let go is built on the way our child is shaped – through loving discipline and praise – when they are happy for us to have hold of them.

The older they get the more difficult and painful it is to administer discipline. Working hard at learning lessons through trusting them again and again when they are younger should help them to make better choices when they start listening more to themselves and their peers than their parents. It's never too late to adopt this approach but the longer you leave it the harder it will be.

Learning to handle money and how to look after the possessions of others as well as our own is another important trust infused learning phase. Trusting them probably doesn't mean continually topping up their pocket money when they spend it all within hours of getting it. However, it does involve talking through the consequences of them doing this, letting them experience the consequences and then giving them the money again when it's due next week.

Perhaps your child breaks your iPad screen? Putting sensible restrictions and supervision around using such a valuable piece of kit enables you to continue to trust them with its use, and for them to rebuild our confidence in them using it by themselves at a later time. But it may be that they are just too young for that level of responsibility so don't set them up to fail in the first place by letting them use it.

I remember my teenage son treading on the laptop he had left on the floor by his bed and smashing the screen. The fact that he did this jumping up to answer the front door to me (when I was in a hurry and had forgotten something) helped in my decision to pay for a repair. But it didn't stop him from feeling remorse and learning the lesson about not leaving things that break on the floor.

I could have asked for a financial contribution from him and he did offer to pay but it was our judgment as parents that we would not only continue to trust him with responsibility for the kit, but demonstrate kindness in footing the bill. However, if it happens again our trust in him wouldn't be compromised by asking him to pay. In fact it would underline his sense of our confidence in him taking responsibility as an emerging adult.

Setting expectations around the time we want them back following a night out is a good example of how we teach our children about trust. If we say 11 and they get in at 11.30 we may still trust them to go out the next time but curfew is now set at 10.30. Of course, we should tell them that will be the consequence before they decide to stay out beyond 11! Our children generally did get in by 11 and when we said one evening, 'You can stay out until 12 tonight,' you could see the pleasure in their faces. Not because of all that they could do in that extra hour but because they knew we trusted them.

There was one occasion though when my daughter was very late back and it was one of the first times she had been out with a new boyfriend. I remember tracking her down through calls to her friends as she wasn't answering her mobile and then turning up outside the house where she was. Oh dear!

We will stumble through a number of events like this with our Dad-sized boots on, but what happened was that the relationship we had built up with our daughter in the small things over the years meant that we trusted and respected each other enough to talk through the event and both learn lessons for the future. It also helped me to start building trust in the young man who six years later would become her husband.

There are no easy answers when it comes to trust and in particular where the trust has been abused. Some friends of mine have recently confiscated their son's mobile phone because he was misusing it to download unhelpful images and then sending them on. Since this action he has responded very positively and become more sociable and happy around the home with the engrossing distraction of social media and texts removed from his life. However, they know that one thing is for certain – at some point he will ask for the phone back and what then?

I don't know the answer and they probably don't at the moment but they are talking about it not only with each other but also their son. They are taking a long-term view of trust that leaves room for quite severe sanctions in the short term to help their son develop the self-control he needs to make responsible and productive use of this technology. In turn it seems that their son trusts them in this situation and that can only be as a result of him knowing through experience with smaller issues, that they have his best interests at heart.

I really do believe that:

THE ONLY WAY TO MAKE OUR CHILDREN TRUSTWORTHY IS TO TRUST THEM.

You may think that they won't get things done as well as you but you may be surprised. I remember my youngest daughter being placed in a science set at school that meant she wouldn't be able to take the higher paper.

I was all prepared to go into school to do battle and get her moved up but she asked me to leave it to her. She didn't move set but persuaded the teacher to agree to enter her for the higher exam. She then came home and asked me to buy the appropriate revision books before working her way to an 'A-grade' pass.

If I had intervened I would not only have deprived her of a confidence building life lesson but also very possibly ended up with a solution that didn't deliver a result as high as she achieved.

She's still a determined and independent young lady by the way!

And finally…

As we trust our children and work through the various life events with them we will also be teaching how they can build trust with others. Dad may always trust but others may not be so easily persuaded.

If they marry, their future partner will say to them, 'All I have is yours,' and your son or daughter will want to say the same thing back because they have learned from Dad and Mum how to trust another.

At work, their boss will delegate an important assignment to them but first that supervisor will have taken time to watch how they handled smaller responsibilities, building trust in their character and capability. Your child needs to understand how and why that works.

Trust is at the centre of any successful relationship because trust is at the heart of commitment. Dad always trusts because you can do nothing else when your love commits you absolutely to your children.

What will change?

1. Talk with your partner about how you demonstrate trust for your children. Be honest about where you have and are still finding it hard to trust them and work out ways of rebuilding that confidence. Involve your child in finding a way forward once you have talked ideas through yourselves.

2. Have another chat with your partner about areas where you are finding it hard to let go of them, not necessarily because you don't trust them but perhaps because you're worried about the actions of others. Talk this through again with your child and involve them in taking responsibility for coming up with ways to avoid difficult situations. They are much more likely to follow strategies that they have come up with themselves.

    Try to do this when things are calm and well in advance – trying to work these things out when they're due to leave in ten minutes won't work!

Dad always hopes

I'm not talking here about the somewhat wistful hope in, 'I hope they turn out alright in the end'. Dad's hope is a much stronger currency than that.

Our children's rides, particularly through their teenage years, will be like a rollercoaster – their emotions and self-confidence will go up and down with opposing extremes sometimes reached within the same day. Our role isn't to grab hold of the back of their seat and hang on for dear life as they take every turn and plummet, although it may sometimes feel like that! No, our role is to be the supporting structure around their ride.

When you watch a rollercoaster you naturally focus on the vehicle as it speeds around the track. You don't tend to look at the structure of the track (although nervous parents may) because it's just there: solid, immovable, a little bit of where required, but safe, reliable and secure. However, without it the cars wouldn't get far, if anywhere; they would just fly off.

It's easy for our children to look to a bright future when things are going well but far more difficult when the immediate scenario is disappointment and failure. As a Dad we shouldn't be like that. In fact, our 'always hoping' belief in them needs to kick in at exactly the time our child's own self-belief hits rock bottom.

This is how it may look if you were explaining this as a statistician!

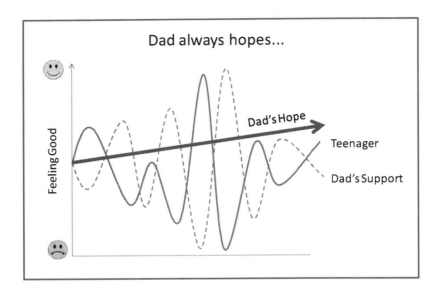

Because we take a conscious decision to 'get in the helicopter' and take the long-term view, we can bring a positively realistic perspective to what seems the worst disaster to our child (and perhaps even to us) at the time.

We can still be involved when they feel good but these are the times where we can take more of a back seat even though we may celebrate with them and help create positive memories that they can fall back on when the going gets tough.

These are the types of lessons you help your child to learn when you're with them through their darkest and scariest times:

- **That they are uniquely valuable** – there is no one else quite like your child. They are uniquely equipped to live a fulfilling life that does both them and those around them good. They also need to hear you say this to them and believe it.

- **That when a door closes another will invariably open** – this is particularly applicable at exam results time or where they face redundancy for the first time. There really can be a silver lining to every cloud!

- **That you don't suddenly become a poor manager, administrative assistant, plumber or whatever you do** – I've already talked about the nonsense of 'you are as good as your last set of results'. We will all suffer setbacks and criticism in the short-term but these are the times when we learn and grow the most but it's also helpful for them to learn how to…

- **…Remember the good times to help keep the present in its proper perspective** – this is where their record of achievements comes in, or even simple things like the list of positive descriptions from the simple exercise I suggested in 'Dad doesn't delight in evil but rejoices with the truth'. You will probably need to remind and help them to do this as it's not easy to remember good things about yourself when the pressure is on.

- **Finding something difficult doesn't automatically mean that you give up** – it's sometimes right to persevere. Re-take exams for example, and even when your child seems to be the only one remaining true to their hope for the future that doesn't necessarily mean they are deluded. What's the harm in supporting them whatever they decide, even if we disagree?

- However...**Sometimes it is a signal to adjust their plans and change direction** – I always wanted to work in medicine but after a difficult first year of A-levels I had to just accept that I struggled with the sciences. With support from my parents I changed college as well as starting afresh with some very different subjects and suddenly I was near the top rather than the bottom of the class.

- **Experiencing and coming through tough periods enables you to be aware of and help others in a similar situation** – when we hit problems it brings us face to face with our own humanity and enables us to empathise with others. It helps to build self-confidence as we see there is a way through, but at the same time fosters humility because they learn that...

- **...It's OK to ask for help** – there are few things in the workplace that annoy a boss more than someone not asking for help when they need it. It causes much more trouble sorting out the resultant mess. It's the same in families – how many times has a husband or wife tried to hide the consequences of overspending from each other? It's much better to be honest and work out a solution together. And when they're still children at home with us we absolutely want them to come to us for help and guidance without fear of us being disappointed in them.

- **It normally takes time, dedication and patience when it comes to fulfilling hopes** – our children are constantly subjected to the 'get rich quick' culture and so-called 'reality TV' driven cravings for instant fame. They're sometimes unhelpfully labelled as being a member of the indulged 'Me' generation where they expect everything to fall into their laps. Our children aren't stupid and will recognise that TV presents a very narrow view of reality as do the substantial starting salaries that are secured by the very few on accelerated graduate schemes.

If your child gets onto one of these, well done and good luck to them – they will not only have the required talent but also would have worked very hard. But there are so many other paths through life and there is much happiness to be found in being content with hopes and dreams not just being defined by progression in the workplace.

- **That whatever happens you still believe in them** – and this isn't a 'there-there' sentimental feeling but a conviction rooted in reality; that they are your children and are uniquely gifted and equipped to be 'successful' whatever that may mean. Have you ever said the words 'I believe in you' to your child? There will be very few things that help them believe in themselves more than those words sincerely delivered. Also be ready to tell them why.

But please remember that they will also expect to see you at least trying to take the same attitude yourself if your encouragement is to be worth anything. In fact, I've found it quite sobering to examine my own reaction and beliefs in challenging situations as I've typed out these thoughts.

So returning to your child or children, here are some searching questions to consider:

- What are your hopes for your child?
- Are they aligned with their own hopes?
- When was the last time you talked with them about their hopes and dreams?

Even if children have their own ideas about the future they will very often work towards what your hopes for them are, or, possibly more dangerously, what they THINK your hopes and expectations for them are. A parent's actual or perceived expectations can be a heavy burden and sometimes with tragic consequences.

The way to address these potential conflicts is to talk and talk regularly both as parents and with your children. They may find it a bit disconcerting to be put under the spotlight but at some point the questions about options, further education and careers will come up at school. So although that's only one part of their future, it will at least give them a degree of longer-term perspective when deciding on next steps.

It will also help to align your hopes with theirs and give you an opportunity to encourage them to broaden their minds to future possibilities. I remember a young man coming to see me a few years back to seek guidance about his future and when I asked him what he had planned for further education he somewhat unenthusiastically said 'accountancy'.

I agreed it was a great profession to get into but then asked him what his passion was. 'Surfing' was his reply. I was then able to encourage him from my own experience to look into places where accountants worked – his understanding was that they just worked in accountancy firms – and assured him that accountants were also needed in the world of surfing!

He did become an accountant and although not in the world of surfing he enjoys his work and he isn't part of an accountancy firm either!

An interesting thing about this story was that it was his Dad who encouraged him to speak to me because he recognised my experience of the commercial world was broader than his. That demonstrated real humility from a Dad with high hopes, genuinely looking to the best interests of his son. It's OK and often very helpful to involve others when helping our children formulate and then plan towards achieving their hopes and dreams.

And finally...

Your child's hopes and ambitions will very probably swing every bit as much as their rollercoaster ride through the teenage years: from nurse to pop star to vet, or wherever their ambitions eventually land.

Through all of this Dad needs to work hard to understand, help shape and encourage these hopes particularly when circumstances cause your child to lose confidence in where they're going.

We have already said that however hard or far our child falls they should always know they can land on the kindness of Dad. But they should also know that when those times come their Dad still believes in them however hopeless they may think their situation is.

Because there will always be hope, and the one to tell them that and help them take their next steps is a Dad who always hopes.

What will change?

1. Write down the hopes you have for your child – it's a good
    idea to do this together with your partner. Make a special
    and 'do not disturb' time to ask them what their hopes are –
    what's really important to them?

2. Why not make this a regular 'milestone' event – perhaps
    the first meal in the New Year or after each school report!
    Your child should walk away from that table feeling six
    inches taller.

3. Have you started the 'Me' file with your child yet? You
    never know when they will need it to reflect back on and
    rebuild their confidence.

4. Don't try and tackle the big decisions like course options,
    career paths and college choices without help particularly if
    it's your first time. Things have changed quite a bit since
    you went through it! Find out when these decision points
    are for your child and make sure you have them in the diary
    so you can prepare WITH YOUR CHILD and in good
    time.

Dad always perseveres

Perseverance is the last of the 'Always' descriptions and a Dad characteristic that is part of many of the others – Dad should always persevere to be kind, patient, keep no record of wrongs etc. But I want to devote this chapter to something where it's probably more important to persevere as a Dad than anything else. It's absolutely foundational and it's difficult to think of any relationship without it.

COMMUNICATION

I don't feel very qualified to talk about this area because, if I'm honest, it has been my wife who seems to get to a deeper level with our children much more than I do. Perhaps it's a 'bloke' thing but even if there is some truth in that observation it doesn't mean that we can ignore how we communicate with our children. In fact, Dad will need to work very hard at communication; there are few areas where we will need to persevere as much.

One of the challenges with communication is that it's a huge subject – in the Amazon books section today there are 242,774 results! So what can I get into five or six pages that will be worthwhile? Given that it's not my objective to tell you what to think, but to help you to think I've turned this approach on myself. I asked my wife this morning to articulate briefly what helped her to communicate with our children. I will describe what she said and then reflect on how I contributed or not.

1. Create regular and quality times to communicate

My wife was at home throughout our children's early and teenage years but she still needed to be consciously disciplined about creating quality time for them. When they were very little this involved lots of cuddles but I remember how she always used to chatter away to them from a very early age. Cuddles and hugs continued to be important and there is nothing quite as stress relieving than a hug from your child.

Later on it took the form of a wind-down time around the kitchen table after school where she encouraged them to talk about their day. This was easier with our daughters than our son. I once heard someone define the word 'nothing' as something eight year old boys do at school all day: 'What did you do today?'

'Nothing' is the usual response!

In their teens our girls used to come and sit on our bed and talk about stuff when they got in from an evening out. Some of us had to get out of bed in the morning for goodness sake! Again my son was more of a challenge but Anna drove him to and from school several times a week, only 15 minutes but enough time to have him sat beside you with not much else to do but listen and talk to Mum!

She respected their personal space and would knock before entering their bedrooms, but she was always welcome in there, sometimes to tell stories but later on just to listen or perhaps wipe away some tears. Very often this was at bedtime that, for whatever reason, is a time when children seem to be more open and vulnerable.

She also arranged 'one to one' treats – perhaps a visit to a coffee shop or a walk – with each of them, and that's something our own daughters are now repeating with their own children. Craft activities, playing games, even watching a film together, all of these things gave room for companionship, affirmation, correction, advice; in short – communication.

Much of this was consciously planned in and in many ways became a routine although it didn't stop them talking at other times. On the contrary I think it encouraged them to be more spontaneous in the way they shared things with us.

How did Dad do?

I worked long hours and often arrived home tired and distracted. It was all too easy to slump down in front of the TV with my meal on a tray. But I did work hard at getting home at a reasonable time at least a couple of times a week, and it's hard not to give time to the clamouring of young children when the first thing you see as you walk down the drive is their little faces pressed against the front window.

Being part of the unpaid family taxi service was also a great opportunity to chat away even if it was about superficial stuff. It also exposed them to my musical preferences and they all still love a bit of ELO or 10cc when they hear it!

I formed a strong bond with my son through our mutual love of sport, driving him to and watching him play in football and rugby matches. Later on, regular trips to Crystal Palace games that also taught him the value of patience and that winning isn't everything! Did we have deep and meaningful conversations? Not often, but the empathy and understanding is there as a foundation when he does want to talk.

113

I very rarely worked at weekends, took all of my holidays and resisted having a BlackBerry for years. All of this made space for quality communication, but I could still have done more to pin that down. For example, I didn't give enough time to support them with things like choices at college where Anna did most of the work.

But I did often read the bedtime story and we ate together as a family at least four or five times a week – these were both simple areas where I could plug into the routines that Anna had worked so hard to establish and try my best to give 100% attention to what was going on in their lives.

It's funny too how seemingly small things make such a big difference. My eldest daughter told me the other day how important my regular phone calls were to her at university. I used to phone her driving home from work and we would just chat away for 10–15 minutes about nothing in particular. I enjoyed the call but for her it was something more, perhaps just reminding her that although she was miles away from the safety and security of home that she was still very much in our thoughts.

So my overall score? Probably scraping a **7/10** – Good try!

2. Pick your moment carefully for the delicate conversation

This is linked to the last point in that if you create plenty of opportunities for quality communication you have more of a choice when to tackle the 'big issues'. You also have more time to probe a bit and get to the real root cause of any challenge they are facing.

If, however, quality times are few and far between, there is a danger of too much being crammed into too little space as the heat of disagreement and conflict builds. Sometimes, particularly as our children grew older, it was best to wait until things had calmed down before addressing certain areas. So much that is unhelpful can be said in the heat of the moment.

Sometimes communication is very much like peeling an onion. I don't necessarily mean the tears but rather the persistence and patience to peel back layer after layer, and there will often be justified resistance from our child to us doing so all at one go!

How did Dad do?

I did my duty and tried to have THAT conversation about the 'facts of life' with my son, but no one told me that one of my daughters would walk in, sit down and chip in with anecdotes!

I also didn't react well to irrationality – Dad certainly wasn't patient when faced with a tearful and ranting teenage daughter although it's amazing what a few contrite words and a hug can very quickly repair. Just as well really.

I could certainly be accused of putting off the difficult conversation for so long that I never got around to having it. However, when I did I think I was clear and hopefully balanced, and was prepared to listen to a different view.

Overall score I would say closer to **5/10** – Must try harder!

3. Respect confidentiality

My wife is a trained counsellor so she's very hot on this anyway. However, for a child to continue to trust you with their deepest thoughts and challenges, they need to feel completely secure in what you will do with what they have said. I'm not saying that you must never disclose what's said and in extreme cases it may be a legal requirement, but our default setting needs to be to respect confidences.

Anna did share some of the things our children told her in confidence with me but always asked their permission. Sometimes there were things I just didn't need to know and vice versa on the very occasional times they chose to confide in me rather than Mum.

Breaching confidentiality can also be something that happens as a result of over-reacting to or being overwhelmed by what our child has just told us; we just feel we need to talk to someone for support or counsel. That may be the right thing to do but our child needs to be involved and comfortable with the decision or they will think twice about trusting us with other stuff in the future.

How did Dad do?

Even though I heard most of these things second-hand from my wife, I very rarely broke a confidence even if from an adult perspective it may have been funny and worthy of a dinner party anecdote.

Overall score **9/10** – Showing some potential!

Here's something else my eldest daughter said about this. That Anna and I each had our strengths and weaknesses when it came to communicating with her, and it was the two of us working together that resulted in us delivering something like the total package.

There are a couple of points to bring out here. First, we had different and in many ways complimentary communication skills and perspectives. But there is something else - **the importance of setting aside quality time to talk with each other about our children.**

Parents I know who have separated give high priority to this and some perhaps even more so than others who remain together.

Communicating with our partner about our children is probably in the Top 3 if not No 1 spot when it comes to effective parenting. It's the rock of all rocks and nothing must get in the way of it.

And finally...

This hasn't been an exhaustive guide to communication but what we have covered are good examples of where we will need to persevere – again and again and again!

There could well be times when your child will cut you off – you may not even see them for days or even weeks on end – but you should never cut THEM off. The communication channels should always be left open at your end, and because Dad always perseveres you never give up reaching out to or receiving your children whatever may have happened and however old they may be.

Life is too short and your role as a Dad in their lives is too important for you to be 'not at home' when they finally decide to call.

What will change?

1. Discuss with your partner how you make room for quality communication with your children. It's one of those rocks and needs to get into the diary, to become part of our regular routine. Perhaps start with a simple and easy to achieve goal like reading a bedtime story and build from there.

2. Do you have the same quality times set aside with your partner? If not get them in the diary and PERSEVERE with making them happen. It may be that you need a third party to challenge you from time to time on how this is going, to keep you honest, but don't delay in getting started if it's not happening already.

A brief pause for reflection

So here we are approaching the end of our journey through the character and behaviours of a Dad: our 'Dad Definitions'.

I wonder how you feel or what you're thinking. Please don't put this book down thinking that you've failed or you'll never succeed as a Dad. It wasn't meant to be a set of benchmarks that you must live up to but a structure to help you think about how you can be the best Dad you can be.

If you've been challenged enough to want to do something to change that's brilliant and it's never too late to start. However, the longer you put it off the harder it can be, and what damage will be done to your children in the meantime? So don't delay to have a go at what you have decided.

At the end of the day it's down to you to decide and control how hard you work at being a Dad. I encourage you not to abdicate this wonderful responsibility, to leave the shaping and development of your children to your partner or anyone else for that matter.

Your children need YOU and most of all they need your love, the committed and unconditional love defined as patient and kind, that doesn't envy, boast, or is proud. That doesn't dishonour others, or is self-seeking, easily angered and keeps a record of wrongs. A love that doesn't delight in evil but rejoices with the truth, that always protects, trusts, hopes and perseveres.

YOUR love as a Dad, a Dad that never fails, and this is why I think we can say something that bold.

Dad never fails – Part 2

I said I would return to this one at the end and share what I think it really means, and to do that I'm going to use what I've heard some call 'The most famous story ever told'. You may have heard it called the Parable of the Prodigal Son, but in fact it's not about one son but two, and primarily it's about the love of a Dad for them both.

There was a man who had two sons. The younger son spoke to his father. He said, 'Father, give me my share of the family property.' So the father divided his property between his two sons.

Not long after that, the younger son packed up all he had. Then he left for a country far away. There he wasted his money on wild living. He spent everything he had. Then the whole country ran low on food. So the son didn't have what he needed. He went to work for someone who lived in that country, who sent him to the fields to feed the pigs. The son wanted to fill his stomach with the food the pigs were eating. But no one gave him anything.

Then he began to think clearly again. He said, 'How many of my father's hired workers have more than enough food? But here I am dying from hunger! I will get up and go back to my father. I will say to him, Father, I have sinned against heaven. And I have sinned against you. I am no longer fit to be called your son. Make me like one of your hired workers.'

So he got up and went to his father. While the son was still a long way off, his father saw him. He was filled with tender love for his son. He ran to him. He threw his arms around him and kissed him. The son said to him, 'Father, I have sinned against heaven and against you. I am no longer fit to be called your son.'

But the father said to his servants, 'Quick! Bring the best robe and put it on him. Put a ring on his finger and sandals on his feet. Bring the fattest calf and kill it. Let's have a big dinner and celebrate. This son of mine was dead. And now he is alive again. He was lost. And now he is found.' So they began to celebrate.[v]

The moral of this story is a simple one: that the love of the father for his son was unconditional. The fact that the younger son was seriously wayward had nothing to do with it – his father still loved him and welcomed him back in spite of everything he had done.

He loved his son not because of what he had done but because of who he was, and that's what 'Dad never fails' means to me.

The love of a Dad for his children is based on who they are and because our children will always be our children our love for them can never fail.

We will always be there looking out for them, and even if they are a long way off we will still run to them and throw our arms around them. Dad never fails.

But the story goes on to focus on the older son:

The older son was in the field. When he came near the house, he heard music and dancing. So he called one of the servants. He asked him what was going on. 'Your brother has come home,' the servant replied. 'Your father has killed the fattest calf. He has done this because your brother is back safe and sound.'

The older brother became angry. He refused to go in. So his father went out and begged him. But he answered his father, 'Look! All these years I've worked like a slave for you. I have always obeyed your orders. You never gave me even a young goat so I could celebrate with my friends. But this son of yours wasted your money with some prostitutes. Now he comes home. And for him you kill the fattest calf!'

'My son,' the father said, 'you are always with me. Everything I have is yours. But we had to celebrate and be glad. This brother of yours was dead. And now he is alive again. He was lost. And now he is found.'

The older son saw the love of his father in terms of a reward for staying at home and working hard but he had misunderstood the reason and motivation for his Dad's love. We may feel some sympathy for the older son's feelings but the truth is that if our love for our children is conditional it is possible, very possible, for it to fail, to give up. But Dad's love never fails because it's determined by who our children are and not by what they have done.

This is a bit of an extreme example but I recently watched a drama about how a Mum and Dad reacted to a growing realisation that their teenage son had committed the murder of a local girl. Their 'default setting' was to protect, to trust, to hope and to persevere, but after the son confessed to his Mum she did exactly the right thing by driving him to the police station so he could give himself up. However, it was their final words together that struck me:

'Will you still love me?'

'I'll always love you. You're my son.' [vi]

That's what unconditional love for a child means and although very few of us will see our children go that far off track, I have seen relationship breakdowns between a Dad and his children over far less.

We may have experienced conditional parental love ourselves but that's no excuse for us passing that approach down to the next generation. We just shouldn't let that happen.

Our message as Dads and Mums to our children should be very simply:

YOU CANNOT LOSE MY LOVE.

It's the title of one of my favourite songs, and although it was written by a Mum for her newly born child the words still work for me as a Dad.

So finally…

That's how I'll finish this book – by sharing the words of that song with you. As a Dad who's still learning but hopes that these thoughts and reflections gathered over 30 years of parenting will have helped you in some small way with your own journey as a Dad.

A DAD WHO NEVER FAILS.

You cannot lose my love

You will lose your baby teeth
At times you'll lose your faith in me
You will lose a lot of things
But you cannot lose my love.

You may lose your appetite
Your guiding sense of wrong and right
You may lose your will to fight
But you cannot lose my love.

You will lose your confidence
In times of trial, your common sense
You may lose your innocence
But you cannot lose my love.

Many things can be misplaced
Your very memories be erased
No matter what the time or space
You cannot lose my love.

You cannot lose
You cannot lose
You cannot lose my love.

Sara Groves [vii]

125

Notes

[i] http://www.dadsindistress.asn.au/www/home/

[ii] Rob Parsons, *The Sixty Minute Father*. Reproduced by permission of the publisher Hodder & Stoughton. Copyright Rob Parsons 1995. The right of Rob Parsons to be identified as Author of the Work has been asserted by him in accordance with the Copyright, Designs and Patents Act 1988.

[iii] http://www.bettyphillipspsychology.com/id112.html

[iv] *Who Do You Think You Are?* Series 10, Episode 10, 2013 John Simpson. Wall to Wall (production company)

[v] Luke 15:11-32. Scripture quotations taken from The Holy Bible, New International Version Anglicised. Copyright ã 1979, 1984, 2011 by Biblica. Used by permission of Hodder & Stoughton Limited. All rights reserved. "NIV" is a registered trademark of International Bible Society. UK trademark number 1448790

[vi] *A Mother's Son* ITV 2012

[vii] Reproduced with the kind permission of Sara Groves. From the Album 'All right here' © 2002 Sara Groves Music/Music Services, Inc (Admin by Song Solutions www.songsolutions.org)

11070966R00079

Printed in Great Britain
by Amazon.co.uk, Ltd.,
Marston Gate.